Adventures? Why not?

Modeste Herlic

2nd edition
Author's edition
2022

Contributor: Marina Magalhães Gomes
Copyright © 2022 Modeste Herlic
All rights reserved

*To my sister Theodora
for her unconditional love.*

This book is about spiritual freedom, which can be found within.

Contents

Cafe Sorriso	8
The mysterious artist	14
The beginning of a new being	19
Amaro and Clymene	29
The ideal job	37
Carpe Diem	41
Detachment	45
Flying high	51
A job like any other	55
The woman in the café	59
The red rose	66
The woman in the poem	72
Grandma Maria's stories	83
Serving	89
Don Juan of Lisbon	94
Contemplation	102
The way	110
Connecting diamonds	114
A treasure	123
Queen of the home	127
A ship without passengers	132
Mother's Day	137
The poem of the universe	141
Dreaming	147
Love	149

How Lucky!	155
A school	161
In every corner	164
Manifestation of a goal	168
The Inner Master	172
A great African king	178
Beyond the horizon	181
A journey	184
Return for a good action	189
The universe	193
Facing fear	199
A blessing	204

*True service to God is always an adventure in
learning spiritual things.*
Harold Klemp

I
Cafe Sorriso

Paulo's current apartment was ten times smaller than his former luxury apartment. He had lived in a sumptuous penthouse overlooking the sea on Vieira Souto Avenue, in Ipanema. Now his life was different. In his new dwelling, the space was small. In the living room, separated from the bedroom by just one door, there was a small table, a chair and an old couch that had been left by the former resident. On the desk, he kept a computer, a piggy bank to store coins, a music box, several pieces of paper with annotations, scattered money notes and crumpled purchase receipts. On the other side of the room, you could see the American kitchen, where there was a fridge and a stove that had never been used. There was also a two-door kitchen cabinet above the sink with two plates, two forks, two spoons and two glasses in it. Everything was basic in his new home. Paulo had no television or decorative objects. When he moved in, he thought of having one guest at a time.

Under the desk, in the right corner of the room, lay four dusty books: *Rich Father, Poor Father* by Robert Kiyosaki and Lechter Sharon L, *The Richest Man in Babylon* by George Samuel Clason, *The Secrets of the Millionaire Mind* by T. Harv Eker, and *How to Make Friends and Influence People* by Dale Carnegie. Paulo was no friend of literature. However, he was devoted to reading with the greatest interest when it came to economics. That's how he spent his time when he was not working.

These four books abandoned on the floor of his new apartment were nothing compared to the number of works he had read about the secret of financial freedom. In his old office, there was a huge library with stacking shelves. There were hundreds of books, all well-ordered. They were works about the key to success. Having been traumatized when he was fired, Paulo did not want to return to his old office to pick up his belongings.

In his bedroom, opposite the bed, there was a table where he kept some medicine. Near that table, there was a simple wardrobe with its doors ajar, since the clothes in it were thrown carelessly. At the bedside, decorated with a lampshade that provided little light, were two books carefully arranged one on top of the other — Plato's *The Symposium* and Eckhart Tolle's *The Power of Now*.

It had been eight years since Paulo had read *The Power of Now*. This book was a gift from his son on his fortieth birthday. He was so amazed by his son's gesture that he ended up reading the book quickly. He read it, but he did not really read it, for at no time did he hold his breath to realize the depth of the words. In just three days, he had finished reading it. He never wondered why his son had given him that gift. He found the book fascinating and practical for business. Sometimes he was inspired by that book to make his emblematic speeches, motivating his coworkers in the art of trading. The truth is that he never stopped to think about the concept of the "now" outside the matter of money. Paulo was simply a born economist. Everything he did, he did with a view to profits.

On the other hand, Plato's *The Symposium* did not take up much of his time. In fact, what Paulo lacked most was time. The more money he made, the less time he had left. In the schedule of the good professional that Paulo was, there were no moments set aside for exercising, being with his family or having fun.

One day, he started reading *The Symposium*. However, he found the language too refined. This book was a gift from a woman who used to serve him coffee when he was still working at his last job. Her name was Vanessa, and she worked at Café Sorriso, located near his old office. Besides serving coffee to her customers, Vanessa also owned the business. She was a sweetheart, and her coffee had a special flavor. With or without sugar, with or without milk, her coffee was like a treat for the executives who frequented the place. Besides coffee, she also offered her customers hot chocolate, cappuccino and much more. All this was a delight for those habitués to Café Sorriso.

Vanessa was beautiful and charming. She had a heart of gold. She was so considerate that it was always difficult to determine if her beauty was greater than her kindness. Gracious and generous, Vanessa used her words with elegance, humility, and sympathy, enchanting her customers. Gradually and without any effort, she won the hearts of those who met her. All the customers loved her, and everyone delighted in her stories. She had a simple way of seeing the world, and people enjoyed listening to her. Whenever she had to comment on life, she tried to see the good side of things. Everything about her was perfect, and most of her male customers fell in love with her in silence. Those who were married didn't want to lose her friendship. The bachelors desired her in the silence of their burning hearts.

Paulo was also fond of Vanessa. He always went there for his morning coffee. When Vanessa saw him, she didn't miss the opportunity to say: "There is nothing better in this city than to start the day with a smile." Paulo was not good with words, but he was delighted to return her smile. Then he would leave without saying anything. In fact, Paulo never knew how to deal with women, much less with someone like Vanessa.

From look to look, Paulo and Vanessa became friends. They had great conversations as time went by. On rare occasions, they would stick to a simple "Good morning! How is it going?". Despite being shy, Paulo made it clear how pleasant her conversation was. One day, Paulo told her, "Talking to you is an endless delight." Vanessa was perplexed at the time, knowing that Paulo was not a big fan of poetry. Amazed, she smiled as she always did and said in a soft voice, "Ah, my friend Paulo! How beautiful. You've made my day." Vanessa was surprised because she didn't know that love could make poetry sprout in the heart of any human being, whether king or slave.

Little by little, Paulo began to share some of his concerns with Vanessa. On the other hand, she never mentioned anything about her personal life or about her problems. She was content to listen to Paulo's stories. He knew very little about her, like all the other customers at Café Sorriso. All they knew was that she enjoyed life and loved traveling.

Paulo was given Plato's *The Symposium* four years before everything fell apart in his life. It all happened in a routine conversation at the Café Sorriso. It was Paulo's birthday. Sergio, his boss, had given him a day off, to celebrate and spend it with his family. Even so, Paulo wanted to work. He looked at Sergio and said with irony, "I think about the money I won't be making if I stay home." After a short laugh, Sergio replied with satisfaction, "Great!" Then he added with a certain sarcasm, "You're the boss!" They both laughed.

It should be noted that at that time, the need for Paulo to remain at work all the time was not motivated by the search for money, as he was already a rich man. The reason he would rather not be at home was because he did not feel happy with his wife. Moreover, the children had already taken their bearings in life. The truth is that Paulo had never felt happy with his family. Over the years, he came to realize that material wealth was not always a guarantee of happiness. At least he knew the importance of love and care for his relatives as much as possible.

On his forty-second birthday, Paulo, in front of Cafe Sorriso, did not want to pay attention to the day he was born. At the entrance of the Café, was written:

A smile to start the day,
With an open heart,
With nothing to wish for,
Without expecting anything in return.
A day, happy or sad,
A smile that costs nothing
To change the world
And cheer up
The heart of the unknown.

For years, Paulo had come across this message, but he had never been able to read it completely. He didn't have much time to waste on things besides work. He behaved the same way even on his birthday.

Before entering the Cafe, he looked at his watch. It was seven thirty. He always arrived thirty minutes before his office opened. That way, he could spend some time with Vanessa.

— Good morning, Vanessa! How's everything here today?

— Too early to tell. So far, so good! What about you?

— I'm fine too! I need a coffee from Cafe Sorriso to start the day.

— Oh! How nice. The taste of coffee is magical when the customer's heart is joyful.

— But you know, I haven't been cheerful lately. Anyway, I'm sure I'll enjoy your delightful coffee that never disappoints.

— What happened?

— It was no big deal. Stuff happens.

— I saw on Facebook that it's your birthday today.

— Oh! It's true!

— Happy Birthday! I wish you peace, love, and much success in this new cycle. You should have stayed home to enjoy your day and celebrate with your loved ones.

— My colleagues and I agree that time is valuable. We shouldn't waste it on unnecessary things.

— I think you and your colleagues communicate in Chinese. But I only speak Portuguese — Vanessa said with a soft laugh.

Paulo went on.

— It's just that everything goes so fast in this life. If I go one day without working, the company will lose a lot.

— Paulo, my friend, you are free to do whatever you wish. Just don't forget that everything in life is a celebration. So there's nothing bad about celebrating the day we came into this world.

Paulo bowed his head and said timidly, "Men like me don't lead this sort of life." Vanessa responded immediately, "If the world of success is like this, I don't want to live in it."

— You're right. It's just that success is not always for the romantics — said Paulo.

— Anyway, I have a gift for you.

Vanessa bent down and got something from the other side of the counter. Then she gave him the gift wrapped in golden paper, tied with a red bow. Paulo thought about love. He took the little present and opened it immediately. It was Plato's *The Symposium*, a beautiful text on the meaning of love and friendship.

— Wow! — exclaimed Paulo.

— What's surprising about that? — asked Vanessa.

— Are you giving a book written by a dreamer to a pragmatic man like me?

— Yes, I believe in change.

— That was a good one — Paulo agreed, smiling. — Anyway, thanks, Vanessa!

— I'm the one who should thank you.

His watch beeped. It was eight o'clock. Paulo said goodbye and left in a hurry. A lot of work was waiting for him.

II
The mysterious artist

In the bedroom of Paulo's new apartment, there was a small, simple dresser placed near the entrance to the bathroom. In it, there was an unfinished illustration of a shack in the middle of the forest. Paulo had kept this drawing since he was six years old.

In addition, there was a work of art. It was an acrylic painting called *The Return*. It represented a bright star in the middle of a bluish sky. At the star's edges, the work was darker and marked by a gradual change in tone. From the left corner at the bottom of the canvas, there was a golden path that went toward the star. The cool color of the painting promoted a feeling of peace and serenity in the heart of those looking at it. However, Paulo never stopped to contemplate this painting. This small picture was the only work of art he had in his apartment.

In the summer of 2001, Paulo and his family went for a walk at General Osorio Square in Ipanema. That day, in that same place, the Hippie Fair was happening. Rafael, Paulo's youngest son, who was the Soul of a poet, was only nine years old. While his family was walking in the square, the boy saw an artist, who not only created and recited poems, but also sold paintings.

"Dad, I want to hear that poem", cried the boy. Paulo, his wife and the two children went to the poet. When they got there, they realized the artist's miserable condition. However, he seemed to think himself rich. Maybe it was because you must have the wealth of your heart to write or recite a poem. Paulo put a coin in the glass bowl. The artist, sitting down, looked at them and said eloquently, "Under the sun, I speak to myself, singing the melody of life. I see what the eyes do not see. I say what the ears do not hear. I am what the world does not want to be. Am I a wise man among the mad? A fool among men? Or a wretch among the rich? Oh! Holy Creator, I do not know who I really am."

Paulo was embarrassed. The two kids seemed to enjoy that weird poet. Their mother, astonished, smiled and put three coins in the transparent bowl. Soon after, the artist laughed wholeheartedly. His laugh was bizarre and funny at the same time. The family looked at him, and he looked back at them. Together, they had a cheerful laugh.

Paulo watched him suspiciously, trying to understand his appearance. The poet was a slender man. His countenance, though pale, was illuminated. His smile evoked a feeling of contentment. He was a poor citizen with a very well-cared for goatee and mustache. He was very attractive, even though he was wearing a torn T-shirt. It wasn't hard to tell that his belly was empty. Yet, he seemed satisfied as if he had just eaten. At times, he smiled like an angel, and at some other times, he frowned seriously as if he had many worries.

After looking at that artist in detail, Paulo thought, "If he's wearing a torn shirt, it mustn't be because he's sloppy. It must be because it's the only clothing he owns." After thinking about it, he put a few more one-real coins in the bowl.

The artist did not ask the family what theme they would like him to develop in his poem. He simply stood up with pride and humility at the same time. He stroked his mustache and goatee gently, walking from side to side. With a dramatic attitude, he moved with grace and gestured like a prince in a palace. He looked up at the sky and began to recite a poem. As he spoke, his words rhymed with his gestures. He was in a state of pure harmony.

"I know very little about truth. However, I believe that life is a gift. To live is to be grateful for every moment, every smile, every adversity, every hug, and everything else. To live is to enjoy the journey and not yearn for the destination. To live is to find joy in every step as you go towards the unknown. To live is simply to love, even if life seems to mock us. So live as if everything you do is a consecration. Walk as if you were dancing with the melody of love.

"I say that because the heartbeat is a verse in the poem of life. In the daylight, dance as if the movement is a celebration of Soul. In the dark night, lie down with joy and sleep in peace, free from remorse. Behold love as if you were playing the divine flute. Live every moment of your existence with no fear. Live joyfully and do not fear death. Fear for what? It's nothing else than the night of the day. Breathe in the light air of life and think, 'I love and will always love, for in love I find myself.'"

The children looked in wonder at this spectacle. Little Rafael was so absorbed in the words of the man that he did not even notice when the poem ended. Another artist Paulo knew had already said, "Poetry is the same as life, infinite as the sea. When it touches a man's heart, it is never forgotten."

"Come on, children! The poem is over", Paulo said. The artist went silent and sat down. "No, Dad. I want this painting", replied Rafael, pointing at a work of art. That's how they bought that blue painting from the mysterious artist at the General Osorio Square. A few years passed, Rafael lost interest in the canvas, which ended up with his father.

Deep down, Rafael was a lot like his father. As a child, Paulo only dreamed of two things — to become a great painter and to get to know all the countries in the world. When he was only five years old, he already scribbled in his notebook some natural objects such as plants, trees, mountains, valleys, stars, animals, and human beings. His father was always happy when he came across his son's illustrations. Paulo also sketched things that his parents did not know about, things taken from a child's fertile imagination.

When he wasn't equipped with a pencil, he had a brush, a pen, or a piece of chalk. The truth is that Paulo did not spend a day without drawing. During his vacation, when he didn't have a notebook anymore, he would paint things on everything you could see in the family home, such as chairs, tables, doors, walls, the refrigerator, the stove and much more. He left his artist's mark on everything that had a surface in that house, including the floor. When he turned six, he was beaten by his mother for messing up the house with his flood of illustrations. As a punishment, he had to repeat the following statement fifty times, "When I grow up, I will be a doctor." That day was the last time Paulo ever made a complete drawing. In fact, since then, he never painted or drew again. Being a health professional was always his mother's dream, but unfortunately, she could not join college. She hadn't realized her dream, but she promised herself that her beloved son would achieve it.

Paulo did not do what his mother wanted. In an act of rebellion, he studied economics. As a pastor's son, he also acted against his father's will when he skipped the evangelical seminars as well as the classes in theology. Against his mother's wishes, he did not enroll in medical school. His mother questioned him about this, and he answered that he had just forgotten. At the end, he followed neither his father's nor his mother's wishes. They took a long time to accept their son's choice.

Paulo's second big dream was never manifested. Soon after graduating, he got a position in a renowned stock market investment company. Over the years, he became the firm's greatest economist. He worked there for over twenty years until he was fired. During all this time, he was so in demand for his work that he never had a moment to himself — a moment to travel and get to know the world, a moment to enjoy life with his children and his wife. Now, he found himself alone, facing his failure. He had failed not only as an economist, but also as a family man. After all these years serving the science of money, he ended up finding himself alone in that tiny apartment, far from everything he had conquered and lost.

In the neglected bathroom of the apartment, there was space for only one person. On the sink, just one soap, and above the sink, a round mirror. Whenever Paulo looked at himself, he would ask, "Why me? Why did all this happen to me?" He was reflective for a moment and soon continued his daily routine, which was to come and go without thinking too much. Sometimes the circular shape of that mirror reminded him of the illustration of the cycle of rebirths. He had discovered that expression in a book he had read a few years before. Now he tried in vain to remember the author and the title.

Whenever Paulo took a shower, he would stay several minutes under the water and think about the penthouse where he had lived in Ipanema. He missed his vast bathroom, highly adorned with glittering artifacts. He mainly remembered the crystal tub that sparkled like a star in the dark sky. He also remembered the winter nights when he was immersed for hours in the ofuro tub, reflecting on how to make more success in life. All this was part of the past. Now, Paulo had to face the reality of the present moment.

III
The beginning of a new being

One day in January 2015, Paulo awoke during a dream. It was not one of those nightmares that frighten sinners, nor one of those worries that torment the spirits of the anxious. It had been seven days since he had dreamed of the visit of a graceful Soul. She had shown herself with a delightful voice and soothing words. She uttered only one sentence, which was enough to reassure Paulo's heart. He was freed from the anguish that plagued him on those nights, and since then, he had not stopped reflecting on the meaning of that dream. In his imagination, he tried to recall the visitor's face, but he could not.

Lying in bed and feeling serene, Paulo remembered that some months before, on a night when he could no longer bear the burden of remorse, he had begun to cry in front of the mirror, saying, "I need help from above. Light my path and guide my steps." Now he wondered if that unusual dream was a sign from the universe. Soon after this reflection, he was mysteriously overcome with a feeling of peace and contentment. Then, he convinced himself that he was not alone on the road of life. Somehow, he began to imagine the hand of God behind everything that was happening, whether in his life or in that of others.

More than two hours passed, and Paulo did not move from his bed. The day was beginning to clear up. The sun rose slowly on the horizon, and one of its rays, still weak, came through the bedroom window. Everything around Paulo became golden, including the sheet. It was beautiful to see. Stunned, he got up and went to the window.

At dawn, the noises of the metropolis are asleep. The big city of Rio de Janeiro is like that too. Near the window of his apartment, Paulo looked at the streets, which were practically deserted. Everything there was calm and peaceful. Paulo had always lived in Rio, but he had never experienced such a genuine and rejuvenating silence of Soul. He put his head outside the window and felt the breeze touch his face. Something within him vibrated. He felt a brief agitation, but he could not tell what it was. He simply felt like going to the beach. "Why not go to the beach?" he thought immediately.

Then he took a notebook and a pen and put them in his backpack. He hurried down and headed to the beach. The closer he got to the sea, the more he had the feeling of distancing himself from his thoughts and worries. The beach was ten minutes away from his building. However, time flew by, and he reached his destination without realizing it. When he got there, he stood before the sea. To his surprise, he noticed the sky, which was adorned by a rainbow. The sea, at times agitated, roared like a storm; at times calm, sang the sweet melody of silence. With joyful twittering, the birds took possession of the sky and flew within the infinite blue.

The sea appeared endless, incorruptible by the oscillations of the waves, whether turbulent or calm. The sea was there, full of life. So, it had remained and would remain forever, untouched by the kindness and greed of its human admirers, resistant to any type of intemperate weather.

Paulo looked deeply into the ocean and was stunned, for he had never seen nature in this way. The vastness of the sea brought him a feeling of great peace, serenading his heart. He just stood there in silence, watching the ripples of water that went on and never ended. The pleasant breeze that surrounded the ocean caressed his skin. Paulo's face sparkled, and he felt small before the magnitude of creation.

Then he closed his eyes with humility and, in his heart, thanked the creator. Just as many men pass by beauty without ever realizing it, Paulo had always lived by the sea, but had never come to know it as he did now. Perhaps it was because he had always had a worried mind.

Thereafter, he sat down on a bench by the sea and started drawing in his notebook. The sun's rays had already increased. A new sun began to shine on Paulo's days, and he was grateful for realizing this.

There he was, sitting on the bench, meditating, with the unfinished drawing of the sunrise in his hands. Suddenly, a woman appeared and said, "I've been walking for over an hour to get here. I'm a little tired. Can I sit next to you?"

— Yes, sure!

Paulo was surprised by the woman's manner. People don't usually ask for permission before sitting on public benches. He shifted his things to give her space. She sat down and then took a book out of her purse. It was *Siddhartha* by Hermann Hesse. In silence, Paulo thought, "This book is difficult to read."

It appears that the woman read Paulo's mind, and soon she said, "Not everyone likes this book. Some say the language is very poetic. However, when you read it with your heart, you can see how interesting the story of Siddhartha is."

— One of my friends started reading it, but he soon gave it up. I guess he was not ready for it.

She pondered and said, "Man is like a river. He will eventually reach the sea."

She felt comfortable at Paulo's side, and he also felt happy seeing her. They smiled at each other. Within himself, Paulo had a feeling that he had known her for a long time, as if she were an old friend. She was a delicate woman, with a thin face. Her dark brown hair reached her shoulders. The smile in the corner of her mouth seemed eternal. Through her glasses, one could see her eyes sparkling with joy. She looked like a calm person, always willing to help those in need. With a gentle air, she evoked the serenity of a happy Soul. Everything about her was simple and full of life.

Paulo felt that her presence was what was missing from his drawing. He then started drawing the bench where the two were sitting. Shortly after, she looked at him and said, "Wow, what a beautiful drawing!"

— It's the sunrise.

— So you woke up very early today?

— Yes, I wanted to do something different. I got here when dawn was breaking in the horizon. I felt inspired to bring my notebook and pen with me. I haven't drawn for a long time.

She closed her book and said, "You know what? Instead of reading, I'm going to talk to you. And she added, smiling, "If you don't mind."

What Paulo needed the most at that moment was someone to listen to him. In big cities like Rio, it is hard to find someone who is willing to listen. People usually prefer to do the talking. Knowing this, Paulo rejoiced in the availability of this mysterious woman.

— Are you sure? My story isn't the most beautiful one — said Paulo.

— That's why it will be a great pleasure to hear it — she said gracefully.

Paulo then began speaking.

— Where do I start? There is so much to tell. I don't think we'll have enough time.

"We have an entire lifetime", the woman said, smiling. She put the book *Siddhartha* back in her bag, put her hands together and said happily, "I have an open heart to receive whatever comes."

All this was a new experience for Paulo. He was a little embarrassed and couldn't start his story. At his core, he really wanted to share it with her. However, he was afraid because he thought it was necessary to know her better. Sometimes, even with one's eyes wide-open, fear can steal moments in which the universe wants to offer us a caress. In fact, like many other men, Paulo had difficulty in accepting the gifts of life.

Luckily, that woman was no ordinary person. Her smile alone was like a gift, and Paulo could not hide the happiness he felt being near her. With elegance and patience, she realized that all that was needed was a little courage for Paulo to do what his heart wished. So she continued the conversation.

— Do you live near here?

— Yes, I do, not very far from the beach. I moved here two years ago.

— Really? Where did you live before?

— In Ipanema, in an apartment overlooking the sea.

— It must have been gorgeous!

— True! It was a luxurious apartment. I sometimes miss that.

— That's a shame!

They were both silent for a moment.

"The sea is splendid, don't you think?" the woman said in a kind voice, bringing Paulo back to the conversation, to the present moment.

— Yes! It's spectacular.

— The moments of the day I like the most are sunrise and sunset. In them, I feel the presence of God. What about you?

— I don't know the answer. The truth is that I've just discovered that the day is made of moments. I had never thought of it that way.

— Imagine yourself sitting by the sea, contemplating its infinite blue and seeing the sun rising or setting. Meanwhile, the color of the sky changes every second. Is there anything more beautiful than nature manifesting itself in a thousand colors?

— I realize how much I missed in my old life without a moment to breathe and contemplate nature. Now I understand what my ex-wife always said about the sea.

— Would you like to share this with me?

— I certainly would! Her name is Renata. She loved to go to the beach and sit on a bench to enjoy the sea and the comings and goings of people. She also walked in the late afternoon when the sun was no longer hot. She loved to go to the rocks in Arpoador to watch the sunset. At that moment, people usually clap their hands in front of this wonderful spectacle. She always invited me to go with her. Unfortunately, I could never find the time for it.

— Really?

— I sometimes miss her, but I should learn to accept things as they are.

— Everything passes, my friend. They say time is the best medicine. But now, enjoy the present moment. Look at the beauty around you and realize how generous creation is.

— True! Being here presently, watching the infinite sea, I realize that all we know about creation is just a drop of water. I think the genuine truth must be bigger than the ocean.

— How beautiful! Your words sound like poetry.

— Thanks for thinking this way.

The woman came a little closer to Paulo and said curiously, "So, were you born around here?"

— I was born and raised here. What about you?

— I'm from Rio as well. I lived here for 48 years. Then I moved to Canada, where I've lived with my husband for twenty years.

— Wow! How interesting! I am also forty-eight years old.

— I could be your mother.

They both laughed. Paulo started feeling more at ease. Then he went on.

— Are you here on business or for pleasure?

— For pleasure. I come to Brazil every year, escaping the cold in Canada. I'm not a big fan of winter.

— Doesn't your husband mind your traveling alone?

— No, he doesn't. The interesting thing is that nobody ever asks me if I don't mind him not coming with me.

— I see what you mean! I'm sorry! — Paulo said, embarrassed.

— Relax! It's okay! Everybody asks me if my husband minds that I come alone — she replied, still smiling.

— I realize that in our society, we cannot see a woman as an autonomous being, independent of her husband — Paulo was silent a moment. — Changing the subject, what do they think of this beautiful city in Canada?

— That's a good question. Some people think we live, celebrating life all day long. You know, I have a student from Canada who once came to Brazil with me and asked, "Where is the music?" And I said, "People in Brazil don't play music all the time. They lead normal lives. They work, sleep, and do serious things too." It turns out that when he arrived in Brazil, he thought he would be seeing people dancing in every corner of the city.

They had a laugh. She continued, "I'm surprised to see how people invent these stereotypes and believe them!"

— It's a funny and terrible reality at the same time.

— What about your family? Do you have any brothers and sisters? — asked the woman.

— No, I'm an only child.

— Have you ever wished you had siblings?

— Yes, occasionally. It depends a lot on my mood.

— An only child usually wishes to have some other siblings. I have five and can give you one of them if you like.

— Just one is not enough. Four of them would suit me better.

They laughed a lot. Paulo began to feel more comfortable speaking, but just as he was about to start telling more about his life, she received a message. She got her cell phone and said, "I have to go, my friend." When she said goodbye, she hugged him. He was filled with unconditional love flowing inside him, like he had never felt before.

When she was about to leave, she said calmly, "Until next time!"

— I'm sorry. I forgot to ask your name — Paulo said quickly.

— My name is Karina, your new friend.

— And my name is Paulo. I'm pleased to meet you.

— Likewise.

With these words, Karina left.

Paulo sat there for some time. Finally, he got up and looked at the sea. The world around him was serene, and the waves moved as if they were dancing. For the first time in two years, he felt happy with that view of the sea. At that moment, he forgot his troubles and was satisfied with all the grace he received in his life. With this joy, he smiled softly and started making his way back home, enjoying the morning sun. With his olive skin, he was very charming under the luminous star. Is this a new sun in Paulo's existence? Or is it Paulo, a renewed man with a new vision? Either way, at that moment he was no longer the same. Something embedded in his inner self had changed, and he realized it in silence.

In family life, love is the oil that eases friction, the cement that binds closer together, and the music that brings harmony.
Friedrich Nietzsche

IV
Amaro and Clymene

Karina's family has members from different geographical regions. Clymene, her mother, was born in Belo Horizonte. At the age of three, Clymene and her parents moved to Ouro Preto, where her father began teaching Geology at the Escola de Minas. Today, the Escola de Minas has been incorporated into the Universidade Federal de Ouro Preto.

Clymene's grandmother, Louise Jane, was an Englishwoman from Truro, Cornwall. She had come to Ouro Preto at the age of nineteen, when her father, who was also English, started working as an engineer in the gold mines in that region. At that time, Ouro Preto was a cultural meeting place for people coming not only from other states of Brazil, but also from all over the world. The Escola de Minas de Ouro Preto, one of the first universities in Brazil, was founded by a Frenchman, Henri Gorceix.

After arriving in Ouro Preto, Lulu, as Karina's English great-grandmother was known in town, married a Bahia native, Archias Euripides, and they had nine children. Archias had gone to Ouro Preto at Henri Gorceix's invitation to teach Mathematics at the Escola de Minas.

Although Karina was born long after Lulu passed away, she always felt very close to her great-grandmother, as if the two were one and the same person in a distant past. That's why, as a child, she listened attentively when grandma Daisy told stories about Lulu. At that time, she asked her mother, "Mom, don't you think I look a lot like my English great-grandmother?" Realizing that this question was coming from a child's imagination, her mother answered with great love, "Yes, I do, my dear."

Years later, Karina spent some time in London and became convinced of an intangible but profound bond with her great-grandmother. She felt at home in England, as if she had lived there a long time ago. The supposed bond that somehow connected her to her great-grandmother, even though it was hidden in Soul, always remained inflexible and unbreakable in her heart.

The family members of Karina's parents were friends. They knew each other because they lived in a small town where everyone participated in each other's lives. Thus, Karina's parents had known each other since their childhood. Clymene was very friendly with Vera and Diva, Amaro's sisters. Whenever she visited them, she saw their brother from afar. Little by little, from curiosity to tenderness, she learned to like Amaro until the two of them became sweethearts and later married.

Amaro did not like to live in Ouro Preto at all because everyone knew each other's business. There was no privacy. When Amaro was two years old, he had pneumonia. One person learned about it and told another person, who told another person, and so on. In a short time, the whole town knew about it. Later that same day, a wreath arrived at Amaro's house. It turned out that the person who sent the flowers had received the news that little Amaro had already died.

Amaro was a low-key person. He did everything without drawing any attention to himself. That's mainly why he hated the small-town gossiping. So, when he married Clymene, they both decided to live in Rio de Janeiro. That is why Karina and all her brothers were born there.

As for the wedding, Amaro and Clymene got married in another city because, otherwise, they would have to invite the entire town. The two families had a brilliant idea. They decided to have the wedding in the Basilica Cathedral of Nossa Senhora da Conceição

Aparecida, in the State of São Paulo. The bride and groom's families were aware that even if they invited many people, few could actually attend the wedding, since Aparecida is far from Ouro Preto. So, they invited everyone in town, but only a few members of the two families and their closest friends attended.

Amaro and Clymene were part of a Minas Gerais traditional family, also known as the TFM. What most characterizes the TFM is the fact that the parents are very strict, quite traditional, and deeply conservative in relation to moral and religious values. Moreover, they like to have many children, and when they don't, they are seriously worried.

Three years after getting married, Amaro and Clymene had not yet had any children. So, as good Catholics, they made a promise to God, "If we have children, the first boy will be called Joseph and the first girl Mary." Three years after they committed themselves to Divine Grace, they began to have children. They opened the floodgate and did not want to stop anymore.

They had six children. Karina was their fifth. It was a great position for her because her parents were already tired of taking care of children, saying what they should or should not do. Although her parents were very strict in some aspects, Karina's daily life had no pressure. She felt as free as a bird, enjoying great moments in her childhood.

At that time, she played in the street with her brothers and sisters and friends. She used to walk joyfully in the wooded streets of Botafogo, where they lived. At other times, she rode her bike and rollerblades. Every so often, she would watch the boys playing soccer in the street. It is worth noting that at that time, there was not much drug trafficking in Rio. Occasionally, a car would pass by while the children were having fun in the street. When that happened, the kids would quickly say, "Heads up! There is a car coming." Everyone would get out of the middle of the street, and the car would go by.

This was a time when children enjoyed the freedom to play and walk the streets without being afraid of anything. Parents didn't worry much about their children's freedom either. In this way, children learned very early on to be responsible for themselves. It was a different era, when danger was rare on the streets, a period when mistrust did not imprison human relationships. But time passes and things change. The hard thing is when they get worse without being noticed.

Clymene came from a family where many cousins married each other. Because of these marriages within the family, there were some weird members. They were people who didn't like to leave home and locked themselves in their bedrooms for hours. Fortunately, Clymene was a special mother, a fan of the outdoors and a lover of life in society. She was like that mainly because she had not had a very pleasant childhood. When still very young, she had to take care of her siblings. She happened to be an only child for eleven years. Her mother wanted to have more children, but unfortunately, she had several miscarriages. Finally, when Clymene turned eleven, her brother Frederico was born, and her mother started asking her to take care of him. Three years later, another brother named Vinicio was born.

The best moments of Clymene's childhood were up to the time she turned eleven. This was reflected in her behavior with her children. She did not want Karina and her siblings to do anything out of obligation at the family home. This more liberal way of raising children bothered Daisy, Karina's grandmother a lot. She thought the permissive way in which her daughter raised her children was not good at all. Karina and her siblings grew up playing a lot, without any pressure and without any obligations.

For some reason, Clymene was afraid her children would turn out like the odd people in her family. One night she gathered her children and said to them with a smile, "You should get out of the house, talk to new people, go to parties, have fun with the beauties of nature, enjoy life and get to know the world. This is how you live well, my dear ones." For her, a child ought to stay out of the house and celebrate the joys of youth. She allowed Karina and her brothers to play in the street. She was very different from other parents, who locked their kids up at home, limiting their freedom.

One day, one of Karina's brothers, who tended to be not very sociable, locked himself in his room for several hours. When Clymene realized this, she called one of his friends to get him out of the house. This mother was already ahead of her time in many aspects regarding her children's education. With her way of seeing the good side of life, she brought out the joy of living and lit the flame of curiosity in their hearts, always exhorting them to be more extroverted.

Karina grew up in a huge house in Botafogo. When she turned twenty-seven years old, her parents sold this house and moved to Copacabana. As the years went by, she enjoyed visiting her old family home and rejoiced in the good memories that remained in her heart. She always knew that the best way to live was in knowing how to keep the best part of her experiences in her heart. On the other hand, when the experiences were painful, she knew how to let go of the pain, physical or emotional, and was left with only the lessons of life. It is through living experiences that one learns to live.

On a night when the stars gathered near the moon to shine with ardor, Clymene said to Karina, "The joy of living is like a flame that is kept in your heart. So, my child, never let the wind of adversity blow it out. That light inside you is all it takes to live well. You can dream of everything you want, but never forget to take care of your inner light." Karina was very young at the time, but her mother's words were engraved in her memory.

People say that the best way to raise a child is to set an example in one's own life. Clymene was not an average person. She was very different from parents who told their children, "Don't lie!", and the very next day, they would tell lies in front of them. Clymene not only raised her children by example, but she always sought the meaning of love in everything she did. Thus, Karina learned always to live according to the inspiration of her mother's positive model.

Clymene saw beauty in all situations in life, whether they were distressing or joyful. That is why Karina always saw her as a spiritual master. Her father, Amaro, was also a special person, although he was a little more serious than her mother.

Amaro was a civil engineer and worked for the Bank of Brazil Development Department. The most interesting thing about this job was that he could choose to work full time or just six hours a day. He decided to work from noon to six p.m. so that he could spend time with his family in the morning. All of his children studied in a public school near their home in the afternoon. This way, the family took advantage of the mornings to go to a park or to the beach. To make the most of each morning, they would leave home early and come back just before eleven o'clock. Thereafter, they had lunch and each one went on his or her way to work and school. Clymene stayed home. At that time, she didn't have a job.

There came a time when Clymene, having devoted her whole life to her family, wished to work outside her home as a teacher. She had graduated from the Teacher's Training School in Ouro Preto and now, when her children were already grown up and didn't need her so much, she realized it was time to pursue her professional life.

One day, she summed up her courage and shared her wish with Amaro. Being from a very traditional family from Minas, he answered, "I don't like this idea very much, but if it is important to you...." To which she replied, "I really need to do this." Amaro nodded with a diffident look and added, "All right! We'll see where this goes."

Some time later, she won a competition to be a teacher in the City and began teaching in an adult extension course. On the first day of school, when she returned home, Amaro said to her, "I'm very unhappy about this." Clymene looked at her husband with tenderness and said, "I will give it up, since you're so unhappy." They looked at each other with love and sadness at the same time. Amaro felt bad for not supporting his wife in her dream. At that very moment, he found himself divided between the expectations of tradition and his wife's happiness. After thinking deeply for a few minutes, he spoke.

— I don't want to see you so sad. Keep teaching at the school, but with a condition.

— What condition?

— You can't spend your money on the house. I'm the only provider — he said kindly.

— All right — answered Clymene with great satisfaction.

Although he was a special person, Amaro did not think very differently from the social consciousness of the time. Tradition taught that only men should support the family. The women were to stay at home and take care of the children. Thus, one could imagine a good housewife, passive and caring, always available to please her husband and meet the needs of their children. At that time, this was seen as the main characteristic of a typical Brazilian family.

Fortunately, Amaro was a compassionate man. He knew how to put himself in other people's shoes and feel their sadness. He also had an ability for admitting when he was wrong, a characteristic that made him different from his friends. He did not mind changing his opinion when necessary. He understood his wife's needs.

Since she did not spend her salary on household expenses, Clymene satisfied her children's wishes with superfluous things. Occasionally, Karina would come to her mother and say, "Mom, I was invited for a party on Saturday, and I'd love to have a new dress." Without blinking, they would go out and buy whatever was necessary. Besides satisfying these little whims of her children, she saved up a nest egg and bought an apartment in Ipanema. She used that money in a very positive way. The truth is that she was a fulfilled woman, independent and responsible for her well-being.

Clymene found joy and contentment in the blessings of teaching. As the years went by, she became a more open person because she could talk to her colleagues at work. Consequently, her world expanded, leaving her more interesting than she was before she started working. The more Amaro noticed these changes in his wife, the more he fell in love with her. They loved each other sincerely and with the simplicity of love, they looked after their children properly. Karina and her brothers were very fortunate to have been born into that family.

A very interesting thing about this story is that even though Karina and her siblings had the same upbringing from the same parents, each of them had their own way of being and facing life. One night, lying in silence on her bed, Karina wondered what made her siblings so different from each other. Over the years, she realized that Souls come into this world with their respective baggage, and each baggage differs from one Soul to another. While some are born as kings, others are born as servants. "Does Divine Justice coordinate everything?" she wondered.

V
The ideal job

Karina was born in Rio de Janeiro and lived for forty-eight years in this beautiful city before leaving Brazil. Although Rio was a wonderful city, she always felt like a fish out of water.

Rio is known for being a city where people put a lot of attention on their physical body, and Karina, since she was little, was always very pale and skinny. She was totally separated from the ideals of beauty of that time. She tried at all costs to get a tan to look more "normal" and to gain a few pounds to feel accepted by the boys, who at that time liked chubbier girls.

Moreover, Karina was different from her friends, since she kept seeking the truth about herself, a habit that was widely rejected in Rio society. She was a good girl, and she noticed, in silence, that some people found her very naive for not knowing how to take advantage of situations. They confused being good with being silly.

Ever since she was a child, she felt a certain sadness that she couldn't explain. She felt a huge void in her chest. Sometimes she cried at school. The teacher would put her in a corner of the room and ask her, "Why are you crying?" And she would say, "I don't know." Karina didn't know what was happening to her. All she knew was that she felt a huge dissatisfaction at her core.

Being from a traditional Catholic family, she went to church every Sunday since she was a little girl and took communion very often. But at the age of fifteen, she began perceiving a change within herself. She no longer wanted to go to church and began lying to her father when he asked her, "Did you go to mass?" With a simple nod of her head, she said yes. She thought it was better for everyone's happiness to tell a little lie than to create disharmony in the family.

Karina had five siblings, and while Amaro's salary was good, it was not enough for them to do anything extra. The children studied in a public school near their home and could walk there. This school was close to a poor community. At that time, the slums were not drug trafficking centers and some of Karina's classmates were children from this community. Therefore, she learned to deal with people from different levels of society. From an early age, she realized that in essence, all men are equal, and that material possession and physical appearance should not define a person's value. This social insight was the first event that helped forge Karina's character as a person who respected everyone.

Although she did not know it, everything in her life was heading for significant changes in the future. When she was thirteen, an incident determined the direction she would take as an adult. One day, one of her friends, who lived on the same street, said joyfully, "I'm going to study English at Cultura Inglesa." Then another friend said, "I'll ask my mother if I can study there too." Karina soon thought about doing the same thing, thinking that maybe she would get a negative answer when she asked her mother. But to her surprise, Clymène consented immediately.

Without much effort, and taking the study of English for fun, Karina studied at Cultura Inglesa for seven years, passing the University of Cambridge Proficiency Exam. Later, graduating as an English and Portuguese teacher and translator, she used her English skills to work as an international flight attendant for five years. This hiatus in her teaching career served as a bridge in her search for her true identity. When she retired at forty-eight, speaking English fluently helped her a lot when she decided to live in Australia and later in Canada.

Another important fact in Karina's life was that Amaro, trained as an engineer, had discovered his vocation for medicine very early. But because there was no medical school in Ouro Preto, he had no choice but to study engineering. But his desire to practice medicine lasted all his life. He became interested in homeopathy, and whenever someone in the family felt some pain or discomfort, he would consult a homeopathy guide and have the prescription filled in a homeopathic pharmacy near their home. Thus, Karina grew up with no antibiotics nor any other drugs that would cause side effects. Later, as an adult, Karina would look back at all the blessings she had received from choosing to be part of that family.

In parallel with the last years at Cultura Inglesa, Karina attended a teacher's training course and graduated as a primary school teacher. At the age of seventeen, she began teaching at a public school in Bras de Pina, a suburb of Rio. She liked to teach, but being a nanny for undisciplined students was something she could not identify with at all. One day, after working as an elementary school teacher for three years, Karina came home and said, "Mom, I'm not a teacher; I'm a martyr!" Her mother immediately suggested that she quit.

Knowing what we don't want and what we don't like is vital in serving life and in finding happiness. That was her first step. Soon after leaving that first job, Karina started teaching a language course as an English teacher. The students were teenagers, and on the first day of classes she heard the guidance of her inner voice, "Show them you are a friend and not an enemy. Be on their side." And so, during her classes, she was able to enjoy some very pleasant moments with those teenagers.

However, dealing with teenagers wasn't her cup of tea either, and Karina then started giving private lessons to adults. Of course, some of these older students had many more difficulties in learning than the children and the teenagers, but the fact that they paid from their pockets and had an inner motivation weighed heavily. What a relief not having to deal with discipline! She soon realized that, for her, this was the ideal way to earn a living, making good friends with her students and having lots of fun.

VI
Carpe Diem

Although Karina had been working as an English teacher for some time, she wanted to have the experience of everyday life in an English-speaking country. She felt that this would enable her to give her students better lessons. In 1972, after some frustrated attempts, she took advantage of her vacation to take an English course in London. The frustrated attempts of previous years were mainly because Karina broadcast to all four corners, she would go to England on her vacation. But eventually, her trip did not come about. So she later decided not to talk to anyone about it and planned her trip without announcing it — and her trip came to pass.

Some people believe that our plans do not work out because of the evil eye. Karina knew deep down in her heart that it was because the energy was dissipated when she talked a lot about something she would like to do in the future. So, early in life, she learned to follow the law of silence and save the energy for specific plans.

At school in London, with students from all over the world, there was another Brazilian girl called Eliana, who needed to work to support herself while studying English. One day, she approached Karina and said, "Hi, Karina! I know you can communicate in English very well, and I need your help to get a job. It's just because I can't communicate with the employers. Could you call this number and talk to them on my behalf? You can tell them you saw the number in a newspaper, that your name is Eliana, and that you are interested in the job."

"Okay! Fine!" answered Karina without batting an eyelid. She called the number in the paper and spoke to a lady who was happy and excited about her English. It was an au pair job, which consisted of staying in a family home to take care of a child and help with whatever was necessary. In return, she would earn some pocket money for her daily expenses. The good thing about being an au pair was that she did not have to spend money on accommodation and food.

Julie, the lady who needed an au pair, asked Karina to be at her house for an interview at 5:00 p.m. the next day. Karina thought she had finished helping Eliana at that point, but she soon realized otherwise. Eliana asked her, "Please! Come with me because I won't be able to communicate with the lady during the interview." Karina couldn't say no. There they went the next day for the interview. When Julie opened the door, she was surprised to see two people instead of one. Karina then explained that she was only accompanying her friend, who was unable to communicate in English very well.

Julie kindly told them, "I need an au pair because I usually spend the day away running several errands. The problem is that I can't leave my son with someone who can't ask for help in an emergency."

Then she turned to Karina and added, "What about you? Wouldn't you like to be an au pair?"

Karina had to return to Brazil in March to continue teaching English, but her inner voice led her to ask, "Can I give you an answer tomorrow?"

Even though she was already twenty-five, Karina still had to ask her parents' permission to extend her stay in London. She called them, and they said, "If you want to do that, that's fine." She then decided to accept this experience that life was offering her. Seize the day! And Eliana got a job helping an old couple. In the end, everything worked out!

The man in this family where Karina was an au pair was twenty-eight years old, his wife twenty-seven, and they had a two-year-old son. Their house was in a suburb in the northern part of London. The couple also had an apartment in the south of France, in a town called Juan-les-Pins. In May of that year, the family, and Karina spent three weeks there, where everything was stunning. The perfume of the flowers was enchanting. The sky was clear, and the birds brought joy with their chirping to all those who were nearby. Karina enjoyed the opportunity to get to know this special place and use the few French words she knew.

She remembered her first French class when she was ten years old. After asking Karina to read some simple sentences, the teacher asked her, "Have you ever studied French?" Karina said that was her first class and noticed a hint of disbelief on the teacher's face. Now she was having this experience in the French Riviera and had a sense of déjà vu. She wondered why.

Karina stayed with this family for five months, from February to June. In that time, she improved her English and got to know two new cultures, new at least in her present life. In July, she took an English teacher's training course in London before returning to Brazil, feeling more prepared to resume classes.

On the flight back to Brazil, the crew serving dinner to the passengers caught Karina's attention. All of them had a good appearance, and it was easy to imagine the glamorous life they were leading, flying from city to city around the world. Karina simply thought, "Gee! It would be a good idea to be a flight attendant." It was a passing wish, which would later come true.

People are never the same when they come back after getting to know other places and other realities. In London and the French Riviera, Karina had felt as if she were at home, and on returning to Rio, the void in her chest and feeling a fish out of water intensified.

Having fun on the beach and other amusements in Rio was very superficial for her, but she knew that in due time, she would find a way of life that would satisfy her. Meanwhile, Clymène was worried about her daughter. She thought she was going through a spell of depression and decided to take her to a neurologist. He prescribed some medication, and within a short time, life seemed to go back to normal.

One day, when everything seemed to be going well, she stopped and thought, "If this medication can make me happy, there must be something different that can also put me in this positive state." From one day to the next, without her mother's approval, she stopped taking her medication and started looking for that something whose name she did not know, but that she knew existed somewhere.

This particularly difficult moment for Karina was actually the beginning of her spiritual life. There are always two ways to see a difficulty in life — it can be the end of a journey or an opportunity to start over. And that was the beginning of a life of many adventures.

VII
Detachment

Many things changed in Paulo's life since he met Karina the Sunday before. After meeting her, he tidied up his flat, went to the supermarket and bought some groceries. He no longer bought take-out food. He started cooking at home and was more and more amazed at the taste of his food. Meanwhile, every morning after his first talk with Karina, he would go to the beach and sit on the same bench, waiting for her to appear. When they said goodbye the day they met, Karina had just said, "See you next time!" He did not have the courage to ask what day the next meeting would be, but in his heart, he felt there was a connection between them and that he did not need to force things. He knew that all he had to do was to keep going to the beach and wait for her to show up.

One day, when the rain in the morning made the rest of the day cooler, Paulo decided to go to the beach in the afternoon. The sea was immense as the universe. The sun's rays caressed his skin but did not burn it. On the seventh day of waiting, sitting on the bench, Paulo watched the people passing by. He did not know why, but suddenly, he remembered his cousin Diego. Then he sensed that his new friend was nearby. He had just thought about her when, suddenly, Karina appeared.

— Good morning, Paulo! How are you doing?

— I'm fine! What about you?

— Everything is going as usual — Karina said, smiling. — What's up?

— Nothing much. It's just that I realize we are very attached to our family. This makes it difficult for us to cope when they pass into the afterlife. I don't think I've learned how to deal with my cousin's death yet.

— Would you like to talk about this?

— His name was Diego. He was always cheerful about life. He never lost the smile on his face, in any situation. My aunt always said that he was the light of our family. And I can assure you she was right, for he did everything so that no one would be sad around him. Because I was an only child, I considered him to be a brother. I loved to play with him. The only thing I didn't like was walking next to him. He was much taller than me — Paulo said, smiling. — When I visited him, we would play and mess around in his house. I was Asterix, and he Obelix. I gave orders and he carried them out. Just the two of us knew about my leadership. The others thought it was the opposite. Anyway, together we were invincible. Our games were always cheerful and crazy. I'll never forget that. We did so many things — nonsense and silly things of all kinds. Our mothers couldn't keep us from mischief. Ah! The good old times!"

Karina just listened. Paulo did not speak with sadness. The memory of his cousin cheered his heart, but he was not aware of it. He paused briefly and continued.

— It happened that when he was fifteen, he went cycling on a rainy day. I remember that he liked to ride fast. In fact, he tried to be like his parents, who were always in a rush. At the intersection of two streets in the neighborhood where he lived, his speeding bike slipped on a rock, and Diego fell, banging his head on the ground. His death was quick, and just like that, he was gone. He didn't suffer much. Of course, we were all sad with the event. You can imagine the distress of his parents crying over their eldest son. They had placed many expectations on him. They were in a state of shock and were trying to understand how they could lose their son so suddenly. It is interesting how life surprises us. Nobody really knows about tomorrow, but I think Diego knew. That must be why he lived happily and left without suffering.

"The next day, the whole family got together. He had already been buried, and everyone was in tears, sitting on the chairs around Diego's photograph. In it, he had an eternal smile on his lips. I don't think anyone paid attention to the joy that emanated from that photograph. Everyone there cried until there were no more tears to be shed. I sat in a corner of the room and hid my face. In fact, I didn't cry, and I didn't want anyone to notice. I believe that the tears remained inside me, and I was suffering at my core. Even today, I keep the marks of that pain under my skin. I can't forget it. Oh! How hard it is to forget things, whether they are painful or cheerful. That day, something not very pleasant happened to all of us. Until now, my uncles do not talk to my father because of this. The years went by, but the sorrows remained, unmoved and insistent, difficult to be tamed. This is what happened: While my uncle was in mourning, totally given over to his grief, my father, a great pastor, entered the room where everyone was crying. Imbued with the belief of saving man from his suffering, he addressed my uncle with the Bible in his hand. He then recited some verses regarding divine forgiveness, trying to console my uncle. The latter, who was already deeply shaken by what had happened, did not want to know about God. To make matters worse, he blamed God for his loss. After listening to my father uttering parts of the divine word with emphasis, my uncle walked away and shouted, 'It is much easier to preach forgiveness when tragedy does not happen to you. What if he were your son? Have you thought about this?'

"My father got silent, closed the Bible, and left. Whose fault could it be? 'He who giveth, taketh away', murmured my father before leaving. That day was the last time they spoke. I don't even think they miss one another. That's when resentment and pride are greater than love. This happens even with pastors. No one is safe from the emotions that ruin human bonds. That's the way it is.

"On the days following my cousin's death, whenever I visited my uncle, I felt he wasn't happy to see me. He expressed a certain hostility towards me. Through his eyes, he seemed to wonder why I was still alive and not his son. He had shrunk in his affliction and could not see that other people were also suffering the loss of Diego. He also ignored the fact that I had once advised my cousin to ride his bicycle more slowly. I doubt that would have changed the course of his life. After all, no one escapes death when it is meant to happen."

That day, Paulo had an insight and now shared it with Karina. "Oh! At last, I have found something greater than death!" Paulo said serenely.

— What? Asked Karina, curious.

— I loved my cousin very much. Death took him away from me, but my love for him hasn't changed at all. The truth is that it got even more intense. Diego was always crucial in our lives. He was like a light in our daily existence. He helped us in everything we needed. Close to him, nobody was sad because he used the words that cheered everyone. On holidays, we played soccer on the beach. When one of us scored, we shouted with euphoria and listened to the waves of the ocean that also roared with happiness. After the match with our friends, he would stand in front of the sea and smile. All this was beautiful to see. At the time, we did everything together and talked a lot. I miss him until now. It's hard not to have him around. Together, we were strong and invincible.

"Years later, I asked my father about Diego's sudden death. He couldn't answer my question. He just said, "Everything in life happens by divine grace. It is God who gives, and it is He who takes away." Then I replied, "If He already knows that He is going to take away, why does He give in the first place?" My father was silent, and then he opened his Bible. Even though he was a great pastor, he needed answers. It was one of the first moments when I began to doubt the church. I deny neither God nor Jesus. I only know that men do not always know the totality of things."

Karina finally spoke.

— You know, your father acted according to his level of consciousness. Instead of being frustrated by his limitation, consider the effort he made in trying to answer your question. It's difficult to find a man who has the right answers to all questions, whoever he is. But the important thing is to be able to detach oneself from the bonds we have created. As for your cousin, it's not possible to get him back. Perhaps now is the time for you to detach yourself from him in your mind. And don't worry about it, for in your heart, he will stay forever. Love is infinite.

— Wow! I had never thought about it that way. Thank you!

— You're welcome!

That day, Karina did not say much. Sometimes it is necessary to forget oneself in order to give attention to those who need to cry or just be heard. Karina knew this, so she listened to what Paulo had to say with love and patience. Suddenly, her phone vibrated. It seemed that she had something to do somewhere else. She spoke before the two said goodbyes.

— Paulo, I must leave now, but next Tuesday, I'm planning to go for a walk in Park Lage. Would you like to come?

— Yes, I would. Great idea!

— Is 9:00 a.m. a good time for you?

— Yes, it is. I'll be there.

Karina left. It was already sunset. The sea was serene, and the waves moved gently. In his mind, Paulo visualized his cousin standing close to the sea. Still in his imagination, he got up from the bench, went to his cousin and hugged him to say goodbye for good.

At that moment, deep in his heart, he detached himself from the idea of his loss. On the other hand, he continued to love his cousin, for he knew death could never stop that sincere love.

VIII
Flying high

After returning to Brazil, Karina continued to look for what she needed to feel fulfilled and happy. After the phase in which she was labeled as depressed, she came to know the sky in a way that was not very usual at that time, mainly because she was part of a traditional family from Minas Gerais.

One day, while eating breakfast at home, she picked up the newspaper and saw an ad from a German airline requesting Brazilian stewardesses. The ad read, "We are looking for Brazilian stewardesses to help South American passengers on our flights. The base will be in Rio, and the candidates must speak Portuguese, Spanish, and English. German is not required." This airline required Brazilian stewardesses to attract passengers who could not communicate with the crew, who usually only spoke German and English. Only a few of them spoke a bit of Spanish, and no Portuguese at all.

As Karina cast her eyes over the ad, she remembered the flight attendants she had seen on her flight back from England. She rejoiced in that memory and thought, "Hmm! Not bad." Without wasting time, she decided to work for this airline. She knew her parents would not approve this idea. They would certainly react negatively, dumping a cold shower over her dreams. In the 1970s, a stewardess was tantamount to a prostitute, so Karina followed her heart and acted in silence.

A few days later, she was called for an interview. Like a brave knight going to war, Karina prepared herself very well, especially in her appearance. One of her friends lent her a wonderful dress, and another friend put a beautiful watch on her wrist. She went to the interview, all charming and dazzling. She was informed that there were eighty-five candidates for fifteen vacancies, but she knew that what was meant to happen would happen. So, having done her part to present herself in the best way possible, she did not worry and surrendered the outcome to the universe.

From that day on, a conversation began in her heart in which an inner voice suggested what was to be done. The perception of the inner voice symbolized the beginning of an intimate spiritual experience, an initiation into the path of life. That sound, soft as dew and sweet as honey, began to accompany her everywhere. It also guided her in everything she did. From that moment on, she started calling this inner voice the Inner Master.

Whenever she listened to the Inner Master, Karina, as Soul, was serene, whether in times of adversity or joy. This Master was always with her, at every moment, in thought, action or repose. Unlike those who let their lives be guided by fear, she made decisions according to this inner wisdom, the intelligence of the heart.

A few days after this first interview, she received a call from the airline inviting her for a second conversation with the interviewer, who said, "Karina, we have already chosen fourteen girls, and you will be the fifteenth. However, the result of your psychological test shows that you are a somewhat introverted person. You need to be more extroverted." Karina immediately agreed, "It's a deal! I can do that."

When she was already scheduled to take a training course in Germany, she broke the news to her parents. Clymène just smiled, preferring silence to words. Knowing that there was nothing he could do because the decision had already been made, Amaro said, "My daughter, from English teacher to stewardess, you are going backwards." To what Karina replied, "I know that, Dad. But I just want to get to know a little of the world. I will only do this for a few years."

While Karina was smiling, Amaro was trying to hide his discontent. A few seconds passed, and no longer being able to resist that smile, he was won over by his daughter's enthusiasm. She added gently, "You can rest assured, Dad. One day, I will teach English again."

Karina felt fulfilled as a teacher, but in addition to that, she liked the idea of traveling to different countries and getting to know other cultures. The values of the people in Rio did not match hers, and she intuitively knew that by getting to know the values of some other cultures, she would find the guiding light to what she was seeking.

There was a situation on board with the Germans arising from a small culture shock. The Brazilian flight attendants smiled and talked to everyone, while the German stewardesses were more serious and reserved. When they saw the passengers so at ease with the Brazilians, they seemed a bit jealous and had a somewhat arrogant attitude. However, this served as an opportunity for Karina to strengthen herself in difficult situations. She also concluded later that this animosity could derive from past karma, from this current life or others.

Flights in South America always left from Rio, bound for São Paulo, Montevideo, Buenos Aires, Santiago de Chile, Lima, Bogotá, and Caracas. At other times, Karina worked on flights going in the other direction, back to Europe, via Dakar, Senegal, and Casablanca, Morocco. Other flights went from Frankfurt to New York, returning to Brazil via the other South American countries. Each monthly schedule lasted about fifteen days.

The work on board was exhausting, mainly because the flights to Europe were nocturnal. After a trip, Karina did nothing but sleep and rest. The good thing about this job, however, was that because of the low frequency of flights, she worked on average just fifty hours a month. This way, she used her leisure time to learn German, French and improve her Spanish. One of Karina's colleagues already spoke all these languages fluently. One day Karina thought, "If she can speak all those languages, I can do that as well." It's remarkable the power of having people around you who serve as a role model. Always impelled by her curiosity, she realized the beauty of being able to communicate with people from various parts of the world in different languages.

She enjoyed this glamorous lifestyle a lot, visiting other countries and friends she had made in several places and learning some other languages. However, something was still missing to fill that void in her chest. That was when she learned a meditation technique that led her to her inner temple. After her first meditation at home, she was amazed at the feeling of peace it provided. How could something that simple give her so much inner satisfaction and joy? Years later, she realized that the emptiness in her chest was a longing for God, and this kind of meditation was crucial in finding God within. It was not necessary to go to any temple built by men.

When she started working for that airline, Karina had planned to do it for about two years. Those two years went by rapidly, and she could not see herself leading the same life in Rio as before. It was very difficult to get out of that kind of work because traveling for her was very addictive. Just the thought of staying in Rio all the time closed her heart, so she knew that one day she would leave. She soon received guidance from the Inner Master. One day, when she had a three-day stopover in Frankfurt, she decided to go to London to relive memories. When she was there, she thought, "It would be so good to spend some more time here in London." The Inner Master immediately said, "Just stop flying and come and live in London again." That's how her adventure as a stewardess ended and gave way to new ones.

IX
A job like any other

Shortly after quitting her job as a stewardess, Karina moved back to London. As soon as she arrived, she decided to go to an employment agency. There they told her, "You are seeking employment as an au pair, but we have something more interesting for you. Would you like to be a chambermaid at a small Quaker hotel, the Penn Club?" Karina was pleased with the offer, as the hotel was right in the downtown area, at Russel Square, near Oxford Street. It was a part-time job, and she could use the afternoons and evenings to study, go for a walk and do whatever she liked.

The next day, she called her parents to break the news. Her father answered the call, and she said, "Dad, I'm going to work as a chambermaid in a hotel. That's what I found here at the moment." Surprised, Amaro answered, "What? Maid? If you really decide to do this, my child, you shouldn't tell anyone." For him, it would be a great shame if his friends and relatives found out about this "horrible" thing. In Brazil, there is a prejudice about certain kinds of work, especially in middle and upper-class families. After listening to her father, Karina replied, "What nonsense, Dad! It is a job like any other." During her stay in London, when her father wrote her letters, he always started ironically, "My dear chambermaid daughter." Karina knew that it was difficult for him to swallow this situation and accepted it without saying anything.

The staff of the Penn Club were mostly English language students from around the world. There was Michiko from Japan, Igor from Russia, Ana from Italy, and other young people from various countries. It was everything Karina always wanted — to have contact with people from different cultures. Her job was to clean the rooms and bathrooms on the third floor. She was able to finish this in four hours and worked hard to do her best. She knew that she could not achieve perfection because perfection does not exist in this physical plane, but she did her work with love. She often received praise from the guests and even made friends with them.

In her spare time, she attended several meetings in different spiritual groups in London. She felt the time had come to take the next step in spirituality. There had to be something that would take her further in her inner contact with God. She visited the Buddhists, the Rosicrucians, and many other groups, but her heart always told her that those were not what she was seeking.

A few years passed, and in addition to her classes and spiritual life, Karina had some love relationships. The most important of them was with Roberto. He was one of her students, an exceptional man. However, as not everything is perfect, the relationship lasted only a few years because of his children. They felt they owned their father, and Karina had the feeling that they thought she had "stolen" him from the family. One day, when she woke up, the Inner Master asked her, "Do you want to live in this animosity all your life?" As harmony and love were priorities for Karina, that was the beginning of the end. Each one went their own way, most probably because they had already finished the karma they had together.

A few years later, with the feeling of a mission accomplished in Rio, the will to travel surfaced again. When she retired at forty-eight years old, she decided to leave Brazil once more. She wanted a change of scenery. But that was not the only reason. It is worth remembering that Karina's desire to live outside Brazil was because she believed she had been her English great-grandmother in a previous incarnation. That is why she was very comfortable in English-speaking countries.

One day, walking along Copacabana Beach, she saw a boy in front of her with a T-shirt with huge letters on his back: AUSTRALIA. The Inner Master immediately confirmed that it would be there where she would live out her next adventure.

Beauty is not in the face; beauty is a light in the heart.
Kahlil Gibran

X
The woman in the café

One morning, a few days after meeting Karina, Paulo woke up delighted. What woke him up was the phone vibrating. He had just received a shy "Hi" from Vanessa, his friend from Café Sorriso. They had known each other for years, but Paulo had never received a message from her. Neither had he written to her. They had just exchanged numbers one day at the café.

While some say that a problem never arrives alone, others say that a blessing is never by itself. In those days in Paulo's life, blessings had come, whether through Karina or Vanessa. Although he did not know this, he was about to enjoy the delights of good fortune. Paulo looked at his cell phone, read the message and before answering, thought about the day he had met Vanessa.

It was morning. Paulo was in his office on the fifteenth floor of a building in Ipanema. Leaning against the window, he looked at the street corner below, where a new café was opening. Earlier there was a snack bar there, and it seemed that the owner had sold it to a woman. Some people in the office said that this lady had voluntarily left the public service. That was all Paulo knew because he rarely talked to his colleagues. Sergio, his boss, passed in the hall, stopped at the door, and said, "The new café is charming, and the owner even more beautiful. Until last year, she worked at the Court of Justice in another state."

Paulo just smiled. Sergio did not wait for an answer and left. The next day, Paulo went to the coffee shop. He arrived very early, at seven thirty in the morning. Café Sorriso was not open to customers yet, but even so, Paulo entered and sat down near the counter. At the café, there were only Paulo and an employee who was tidying things up. She cleaned the tables, organized the counter, and prepared the coffee. She did several things at the same time, and Paulo looked at her, stunned. She seemed to be a strong and independent woman. She was the first to speak.

— Good morning! Can I get you something? — said the woman as happy as a smile.

— Thank you! I'll order something soon.

In fact, Paulo wanted nothing more than to meet the owner of the place. In his imagination, he saw a tall, elegant, and charming lady. Sitting there, he looked at the doorway, waiting for the owner, who never arrived. He then began to observe the woman who was doing her chores, always with a smile on her face. She seemed serene and happy, satisfied with her work. She moved like a doll behind the counter. Paulo looked at her discreetly. It was at that moment that he realized she was beautiful, even more than the preconceived image he had made of the supposed owner of the café. Many pieces of furniture were painted blue, and so were the woman's eyes. That's why her gaze looked like an ocean of love, and, for a few seconds, Paulo imagined himself swimming in it.

Unfortunately, that employee was not the person Paulo was expecting to find. All his curiosity was directed toward the identity of the owner of that place. Anyway, the woman at the café was not a difficult person to communicate with, and she tried to strike up a conversation with the morning customer. However, Paulo seemed a little reticent.

The interesting thing about all this is that even though Paulo did not want to talk much, she took words out of his mouth without much effort. This woman was not only a good-looking person, but also very charismatic. She seemed to be the kind that, when she wanted something, nothing stopped her. In a few minutes, she came to know almost all about Paulo's life, even though he would rather not talk much.

On the other hand, Paulo did not learn anything about her and did not try to. For him, she was just the friendly woman at the new café on the corner. Finally, she offered him a cup of coffee, even though Paulo had not ordered one. He thanked her with a smile.

He concealed his disappointment in not having met the owner of the café. He drank the coffee, paid the check, and left. At that moment, other customers were entering Café Sorriso, and the place was already getting full.

The rest of the week was like this — Paulo would arrive at the café at seven-thirty and stay there until eight o'clock, when his workday started. He stayed there hoping to meet the owner of the café, which did not happen. On the Monday of the following week, he showed up at the café after eight. He was tired of arriving early and getting frustrated. "Since she owns the café, she must arrive later," Paulo thought that day. When he got there, the place was already packed with executives, and now there were two other waitresses besides the one he was used to seeing. He went to one of them and said:

— May I ask you a question?

— Sure! — the waitress replied.

— Doesn't the cafe owner ever come here? I'd like to congratulate her for serving such delicious coffee.

— How nice! She'll love to know this. She's that one over there at the counter.

Paulo turned and beheld the same woman who had served him every day for the past week. He then became embarrassed because she had often tried to have a conversation with him, and he had never been opened to do so.

He only wanted to meet the owner of the café, who existed only in his imagination. That day, he took his coffee and left quietly. The waitress he had spoken with was surprised that he had left without talking to the owner.

The next day, Paulo came to the café at his usual time, very early. The woman at the café was already cleaning and tidying up as always. Paulo greeted her gently, inviting her to talk a little.

— I didn't know that you, madam, were the owner of Cafe Sorriso.

— You can address me informally as before — she immediately replied.

— OK! I would like to apologize in case I was a little rude last week. I didn't know you were the boss.

— Relax, my friend — she hesitated a little. — Can I tell you something I always do?

—Yes, please!

— I always treat people well without needing to know who they are or what they do. That makes life easier, don't you think?

— True! You know, I'm one of those who do things without thinking too much.

— Don't worry. I'm also like this occasionally.

They both had a laugh. They seemed to enjoy the conversation. The woman forgot that she still had a lot to do before the café opened. Paulo continued.

— I was told you worked as a civil servant. Others say you used to be a judge.

— Well, it's something like that — she said with an ironic laugh. — I was an adviser to a judge for many years. But what I really love to do is to serve coffee to strangers.

— Oh! My God! People do invent things, don't they?

— You know, none of my customers ever asked me what I really did — she said, disappointed.

— Changing the subject, could you please tell me what led you call this place Café Sorriso?

— In the Court where I worked, many people called me "Smile" because I was never grumpy. Smile means "Sorriso" in Portuguese. That's why I thought of this name when I opened the café of my dreams.

— Congratulations! You must have taken a lot of courage to drop everything and dedicate yourself to what you always wanted.

— Thank you, but actually, it wasn't very difficult — said the woman with a jovial posture.

— I also think your coworkers at the Court were right. I've been coming here for two weeks now, and I've never seen you without a smile on your face.

— You just have to annoy me to see otherwise, — she said sarcastically.

While Paulo was laughing, she asked, "What about you? What do you do for a living?"

— I am an economist. I work in that building at the end of the street.

— That's great! My name is Vanessa, and yours?

— Paulo.

— Nice to meet you!

— Nice to meet you too.

— I must go now, — said Paulo, looking at his watch.

That is how Vanessa and Paulo met. Many conversations between them followed that day. As time went by, they became good friends and even confided in each other. Paulo always arrived thirty minutes before Café Sorriso open, so they both had some time to talk.

After remembering how he had met Vanessa, he answered her message.

[I'm fine, how are you?]

Vanessa continued the conversation.

[I haven't seen you for almost two years. How have you been?]

Paulo had lost his job two years earlier and was waiting for the next one. He could afford not to work for some time, using the money he had saved for an unexpected situation. Being embarrassed to tell Vanessa he was unemployed, he answered.

[I quit my job, and I'm in something else now.]

[What are you working on?]

[I'll tell you some other time.]

[We miss you a lot at Cafe Sorriso. (Sad face)]

[What do you mean?]

[Nobody talks to me before eight in the morning anymore. (Laughter). But that's okay, I understand. I even thought you had moved away from Rio.]

[No, I just moved to another neighborhood. I live in Copacabana now.]

[Would you like to come and visit me sometime?]

[Sure! When is the best time for you?]

[What about this Saturday?]

[OK! I'll be there! (Smile)]

[Great. (Happy face)]

XI
The red rose

Park Lage is in the Jardim Botanico neighborhood, near Corcovado Hill, quite close to the Botanical Garden touristic site. With its abundant vegetation, Park Lage is particularly distinguished by its cultural refinement. In this bucolic environment, spread throughout this quiet setting with its many hectares of enchanting beauty, are many points of artistic interest, artificial islands and caves, lakes, aquariums, unusual shortcuts, exotic trails, some pavilions and much more.

One feature highly acclaimed by visitors is the exceptional cultural harmony between the artistic universe of the last century and the peculiarities of contemporary art. An example is the architectural style of the palace, which houses an art school and a café. Inside, there are usually exhibitions in which artworks of various genres are exhibited. In front of the building, there is a beautiful garden, sublimely refined by geometric landscaping.

It was a mild morning, and people visiting Park Lage were enjoying the pleasant weather. Karina and Paulo arrived at practically the same moment. They greeted each other with a friendly hug, sat at the cafeteria and ordered something to drink.

— My friend, you seem a little thoughtful today. Are you okay? — Karina started.

— Yes, I am! What about you?

— I'm fine too.

— Do you remember my cousin Diego, who died as a teenager? — Paulo asked.

— Yes, I do. We talked about him in our last conversation.

— I don't know why, but today I woke up thinking of him. One of my grandchildren reminds me of Diego a lot. He is my daughter's son, and his name is Andre. He talks, acts, and plays like Diego. One day, when I visited my daughter, Andre came running to me and said, "Are you leaving already? Are you coming to visit me again?" I got emotional when he said that. I knelt and answered, "I will always come to visit you, my angel." He was happy with my answer and went back to his toys. I was very moved because these words were precisely what my cousin said to me the last time we met. On my way here, I kept thinking of them, wondering about the meaning of this inexplicable similarity between them. Could there be a real but invisible link between Diego and Andre? I've heard some people talking about reincarnation, but I don't know much about it.

— I think it can be a way of seeing certain things in life.

With a puzzled look, Paulo nodded timidly. It was evident that he was not satisfied with this answer. However, he did not disagree or agree with Karina. Within himself, he was unconcerned about the certainty of things. He just wanted to hear more about that subject. Karina realized this and continued.

— I don't want to convince you that reincarnation exists, but I can tell you about an experience I had in this regard. Would you like to hear it?

— Yes, I love listening to your stories.

— I'm glad to hear that. Well, my father passed away in 1980. Three years after his passing, my sister had a daughter. When we went to visit the baby, an aunt of mine said, "Look at the eyes of this child! They are Amaro's eyes." My father's name was Amaro. That was a first sign. My sister worked away from home and left the baby,

Heloisa, with my mother. When Heloisa was about three years old, she went to my mother and said, "Grandma, I am Grandpa."

— Did she really say that?

— Yes, and my mother was very surprised.

— Wasn't that a shock to her?

— Yes, because she was a staunch Catholic and did not believe in reincarnation. She told me this fact in the greatest discretion because I was the only one in the family who held this belief. So, we didn't tell anyone else in the family about this episode. They would think we were crazy.

Paulo laughed, and Karina continued.

— Another sign is that, when my father was alive, he liked to walk with his hands behind his back in front of the building where we lived. One day, a few years after his death, when I came home, I saw Heloisa on the sidewalk near the building doing the same thing. The doorman, who had known my father, looked at me and said, "Karina, look at the way Heloisa is walking — just like your father."

"Time passed, my sister moved to another city with her family, and I didn't have much contact with them anymore. Once, when I was already living in Canada, I visited them on one of my trips to Brazil. Heloisa was about twenty years old at that time, and they followed Spiritualism, believing in reincarnation. One day, we were all three in the room, and I said, 'Mother had a special feeling for Heloisa.' To what my sister asked, 'Why do you think so?' At the time, I didn't know if I could tell them that I thought Heloisa was the reincarnation of her grandfather. And my sister said, 'If it's about reincarnation, don't worry. We are studying this in Spiritualism.' Then I said, 'I think Heloisa is Dad's reincarnation.' Heloisa was in the room too and immediately looked at her mother and said, 'Mom, what did I tell you last week when I said I thought I was my grandfather?' You know, Paulo, my father did photography as a hobby, and Heloisa loves photography too. As a result, she concluded that she was my father. So from then on, whenever I address her, I say, 'Hi, daddy/niece!' And she answers me, 'Hi, daughter/auntie.'

— That's very funny — Paulo said, and they both laughed a lot.

Karina went on.

— I was an English teacher when I was living in Brazil. As you know, teachers are paid a meager salary. But thank God, my father was very generous. So I would come to him and say, 'Dad, can I borrow some money?' He would lend it to me, and I would try to pay off my debts little by little. After a few months, he would say, 'You don't have to pay me back anymore.' So, he gave me a lot of money while he was still alive. One day, many years after his death, I invited Heloisa to go on a trip to Europe. Until then, she had never taken a plane trip. We went to Paris, Nice, and Cannes. Since she didn't have enough money to travel, I told her, 'You can leave it to me. I'll pay for everything.' The following year, I invited her again to go to Canada and learn English. We agreed that she would stay with a Canadian family, so she could practice what she learned at school. She went to an English school in the morning, then we both went sightseeing around the city, and in the evening, she had dinner with her hosts. When I paid for these trips for her, I had the feeling that I was returning some of what I had borrowed from my father.

Karina remained silent, and Paulo spoke.

— I cannot say with certainty that my grandson is the reincarnation of my cousin Diego. On the other hand, I find it very intriguing to hear about your father and your niece. Who knows? Maybe reincarnation is one of the laws of existence.

— You never know for sure. However, it is always good to have an inner perception of the surrounding events.

— It's true! Thank you for sharing your experience with me.

— My pleasure! — Karina said, gladly.

In his heart, Paulo was sure that there was some connection between his cousin's life and that of his grandson. However, he could not find a logical reason to believe this completely. He began to see the law of reincarnation as an existential premise that can be perceived, but not subject to verification. Sitting there with Karina, he weighed several thoughts on the subject. Meanwhile, Karina, quietly, looked at some members of a foreign family, who did not hide their admiration for the beauty of Park Lage. Suddenly, a girl, holding a dozen red roses, appeared next to Paulo and said, "Buy your girlfriend a rose."

— But ... — Paulo replied sadly. He thought a little. — I don't have a girlfriend.

His answer surprised the girl, who immediately turned to Karina. The latter, smiling, asked, "How much is a rose?" Very excited, the girl answered, "Five reals."

The girl took the money and skipped happily away. The rose, however, did not come by itself. It had a little white paper wrapped with a red ribbon. Karina offered the red rose and the note to Paulo. He accepted it timidly, wondering what caused that event to take place. He had been divorced from his ex-wife for two years, and since then he hadn't met anyone who could make his heart beat again. Anyway, the red rose symbolized love, and Paulo knew that things always happened in his life for one reason or another.

A light breeze blew around them. Karina kept silent, always with a smile on her face. Meanwhile, Paulo, thoughtful, desperately tried to find the meaning of the red rose in his daydream. When Karina noticed his concern, she said in a soft voice: "I think it's lunchtime." Paulo looked at his watch, and saw that it was already 1:00 p.m. Then he smiled, agreeing with her. They were at the point of saying goodbye when he said, "Karina, can I have your WhatsApp number?"

— Sure! Here it is.

— Thank you!

— My pleasure.

Karina left. With a meditative look, Paulo stayed there for some time. Finally, he opened the red rose's note and read:

You who are blind at heart,
Who has no eyes to see
The girl at your side,
The girl who accompanies you.
She never falls in love
But loved you at first sight.
One day, you will be emperor,
And she, your empress.
Surrendered to sleep,
In the corridors of a dream,
In a golden palace,
On the walls, on the roof,
In every portrait
The face of your beloved.
You are king, she is your queen,
Love, your kingdom.

After reading the poem, Paulo closed his eyes for a moment. He knew that the person described was not Karina because she was married and much older than him. At that moment, the words vanished from his imagination. There were no thoughts, only absolute silence. With this feeling of pure serenity, he got up and started his way back home.

XII
The woman in the poem

Paulo arrived at the end of the afternoon, right at the moment when Café Sorriso was closing. He never missed his appointments. Vanessa had made herself beautiful and was wearing basic make-up. On her lips, there was a red lipstick like a Cupid's bow. Her nails were painted with nail polish of the same color. With her slender waist, she seemed prepared to win the hearts of those who ventured to look at her.

Paulo, thinking that the meeting would be just a conversation between friends, arrived at the café very simply dressed. When he saw Vanessa, he was embarrassed because of his modest clothes. His face blushing, he tried unsuccessfully to hide his embarrassment. Vanessa was a woman attentive to everything around her. She noticed details that her eyes alone could not perceive. She ran quickly to him and said, hugging him, "Hi, Paulo. I'm glad you came. You can relax. I'm dressed up because after talking to you, I'm going to a party."

Paulo said nothing, just smiled.

She continued.

— Have a seat. I just have to do a few things, and then we can go wherever you want.

— All right. — Paulo said.

He thought they would be chatting at Café Sorriso. However, Vanessa, always with different ideas, had probably thought of something more interesting.

Paulo sat at the entrance to the café and watched Vanessa while waiting for her. All perfumed, she took care of some last things before closing the café. Paulo watched her coming and going in silence. Deep in his heart, he felt enchanted by her, but apparently, he wasn't prepared for this sudden feeling.

The whole Cafe Sorriso exhaled that delicious perfume of orchids that Vanessa was wearing. Sitting there in silence, he watched her, trying not to show that he was interested in her. He and Vanessa had been friends for eight years. However, he had never felt anything like that in her presence. At least, that's what he thought at that moment. And right after having this thought, he realized that he desired her as a lover wants his beloved. He found it a little inconvenient to desire his long-time friend that way for no apparent reason.

In Paulo's eyes, there was shyness, admiration, respect, and fear of Vanessa. Even more important, there was also desire. Vanessa realized this without any difficulty. Thus, she put more elegance and grace into her gestures. From time to time, she would pass her hand through her hair, thus setting Paulo's heart afire.

Deep down, Vanessa also desired him. Perhaps she had this feeling from the moment they had met. However, this was not appropriate at that time, since he was married and had no eyes for other girls. In any case, Vanessa had always found Paulo special. She never said this in words, but she always revealed her admiration in the way she looked at him.

She finally finished what she had to do, and they decided to go to the beach, where they began to walk toward Arpoador. The evening was gradually coming on. The sea was sometimes serene, sometimes rough. From time to time, sudden gusts of wind caressed the surface of the infinite blue, shaking its waves. The sun was already on its way to rest. In the distance, one could see the Two

Brothers Hill and the Vidigal Slum with its lights on, looking like a jewelry box. Somewhere in the sky, neither light nor dark, some golden and stormy clouds were gathering in the twilight. The cool breeze from the sea gently touched their skin. Paulo's heart was cooling and warming at the same time. He wondered if this feeling had anything to do with Vanessa. As he walked by his friend's side, he mentally tried to unravel the secret of the red rose poem.

The poem spoke of a woman at one's side, who accompanied him. And, yes, Vanessa was at his side and accompanied him. Was she his queen? He looked at Vanessa's face and tried to see the confirmation of the poem. Meanwhile, she walked with grace, rejoicing in the delicious sea air, not caring about anything else.

At some point, Vanessa broke the silence. She was always the first to start the dialogue.

— How are things with Renata? Sergio told me that you got the divorce.

— She has a new partner now, and it seems she has gone back to school.

— Really? In which faculty?

— I'm not sure, but I believe it's Business Administration. She has a big potential, and she can achieve everything she wants.

— She seems to be a strong woman. Also, it's never too late to start her studies again, right?

— That's right! What matters is that she is happy.

— True! But what about you? Are you happy?

— Your questions are always very direct — Paulo said, putting his hand to his forehead.

— Sorry. I'm just curious.

— It's all right, I understand. So, you asked me if I am happy. I've been feeling much better lately.

— Any news in your life?

— Not exactly. I've met someone recently, and our conversations are making me feel better.

— What do you mean? A girlfriend?

— No, not at all. I see her as a kind of mother. Our first conversation was a bit unusual, but it turned out to be very intriguing. From time to time, we agree to meet to talk about life. Deep down, I feel that I've known her for a long time. I don't know how to explain it, but I have this feeling.

— I'd like to meet her too. Maybe you could invite her to Café Sorriso sometime.

— Sure.

— That's great!

They were quiet for a while and continued walking in silence. Inside, Vanessa wished that Paulo would take, at least once, the initiative in the conversation. "Is it because he doesn't have the courage, or simply because he doesn't want to talk?" Vanessa wondered. Meanwhile, Paulo looked at her quietly, admiring her beauty. He also tried to figure out whether she was the girl in the poem.

At a certain moment during their walk, the dancing of the sea waves murmured a love song. Of the two, only Vanessa heard it. Paulo was so concerned about the girl in the poem that he could not see or hear the things that only the heart could notice. All of a sudden, he looked up at the sky. Golden clouds slowly disappeared in the darkening firmament. Just after they climbed the Arpoador's rocks, the sun drew in its last ray, and some people applauded the sunset with gratitude.

Then Paulo and Vanessa went to sit a little closer to the waves that were striking the rocks. Vanessa remembered the sweet song of the sea she had heard a few minutes before and sharpened her ears to listen to the melody of this wonderful symphony a little more.

Paulo remained silent as usual, while a thousand thoughts danced in his mind. No words came out of his mouth. In his anxious state, the beginning and the end of the poem were repeating tirelessly, *"You who are blind at heart... You are king, she is your queen, Love is your kingdom."* Paulo sat beside Vanessa, present in body, but not in spirit.

Facing the infinite sea, Vanessa delighted in the waves of love. They brought back memories of previous relationships. She hadn't had much luck in love, but she was happy at that moment.

— Do you still remember your first love? She asked.

— Yes, I do. Occasionally.

— Tell me a little about it.

— It might be a boring story. You already know it.

— True! Your beautiful love story with Renata. It is remarkable how things change in life. Who could have imagined that one day you would separate. When you told me how you met Renata, I believed in the theory of Soul mates.

— I also believed that, but nothing seems eternal in this life. Suffering or happiness. It all ends one day. But, anyway, since you know my love story, why don't you tell me yours? You never talk much about it.

— But my love story is not as interesting as yours.

— Please tell me!

— OK! Here we go. First, I met some appealing boys. Most of these relationships lasted a very short time, apart from the six years I dated Luis. The story with Luis doesn't count because I never loved him. I never really fell in love with him.

— But wasn't there a love story that marked you deeply?

— Yes, there was.

— How long did it last?

— Just a month — she said, serene. — I wanted it to be longer.

— What do you mean? — Paulo, astonished, asked immediately.

In fact, he could not understand how a beautiful woman like Vanessa had no luck in love. To him, she was so generous that no man would dare to leave her. Although he was a grown man, Paulo knew very little about his counterparts. The truth is that most men don't know how to love and praise a woman in the best possible way.

Luckily, Paulo knew how to appreciate women. He saw the reflection of his mother in all of them. That's why he respected them and treated them with admiration, as a jeweler cares for his precious stones. Since he met Vanessa, she had always been brilliant in his eyes. "Only a foolish man would let this treasure get away," Paulo thought, sitting next to Vanessa.

Vanessa went on.

— I loved that man very much. To be honest, I can't forget him. His name is Thiago. Now he lives in England, married to an Englishwoman. You know, Paulo, I get very emotional when I talk about Thiago.

— No problem — Paulo said kindly.

— This story of mine happened just before I went to the university. Initially, Thiago and I were friends and, more precisely, neighbors in the gated community of Aldeia do Vale, where our parents still live today.

— Where is it located?

— In Goiania. Do you remember? I lived there for many years.

— Yes, I do.

— About my friendship with Thiago, the truth is that I had always been in love with him. However, I didn't have the courage to tell him about it. One day, at dusk, we sat by one of the community lakes to listen to our favorite song. It was *I'm Gonna Be* by The Proclaimers. We were there, sharing the same headset. We had put the song on replay in Thiago's MP3 player and listened to it several times. I don't know what came over me, but suddenly, I kissed him. Before that day, I had kissed other boys. However, the kiss with Thiago seemed to be the first of my life. It was as if I were in a dream where everything around me had become bright and perfect. I don't think Thiago was ready for that. He was startled at first, but soon found the idea of kissing his childhood friend interesting. Before that happened, we had been eating a few candies. Mine was strawberry, his was mint. Can you imagine? Strawberry and mint, a wonderful mixture! At each of his touches, my heart vibrated with love and jumped with joy. At a certain moment, he delicately took my waist, and I could feel his hand shaking too. We had always been friends, but at that moment we were young people in love, who discovered the delights of passion. It was twilight. The sun had already gathered in its brightness. Even though I was there, sitting next to Thiago, I found myself in a distant dream where time had stopped. The darker the sky, the more passionate I became.

"A soft breeze caressed us. When Thiago realized this, he put his arm around my shoulder to warm me. I was the queen, and he, my king. I was the lady, and he, my knight. Before us, the water in the lake reflected the twilight. And the love of our hearts was everywhere, in every look, caress, gesture and thought. Love had conquered all that was there. With each passing second, I fell more and more in love with him until I surrendered myself to the prison of his gaze. He was very handsome with his hazel eyes. After I could no longer resist his charm, I put my head on his shoulder. At that moment, I was at peace, and I believe he was too. With this wonderful feeling flowing inside me and filling my chest with ecstasy, I knew that life was worth living. The love that makes the heart tremble touched me. Instantly, I loved Thiago without asking him anything. I loved him without questioning his feelings or thoughts. Then I said to him, 'Now you are my boyfriend.' He just answered with a smile. At that moment, I felt he was everything I wanted in life. I also preferred to believe that I was everything he needed to be happy. He is like you. He didn't talk much. That's why I decided for both of us."

Paulo was embarrassed. He could not say anything to Vanessa because he rarely expressed himself.

She continued.

— You know, I thought my first love would be forever. It turns out that after we dated for a month, he got a scholarship to continue his studies in England. It was all very fast, and he had to travel on a short notice. On the eve of his trip, we agreed that I would visit him in Oxford during my vacation. However, a week after arriving in England, he broke up with me. He said he had fallen in love with a certain Katherine and that she looked a lot like me. He also said that he could not stand to be near her without desiring her because she spoke and acted like me. And I wondered at the time how she could speak like me if we did not communicate in the same language.

"He fell in love with a person whom he said looked like me. Today, she must look different because I, myself, have changed a lot. He justified the breakup as if my resemblance to Katherine was my fault. I tried to make him come back to me, but some days passed, and he stopped answering my e-mails. I believe he would rather not ruin his new relationship. Today, Thiago and that girl are married and have two children. I am happy for them. When I went to England to visit them, the two children called me Auntie Vanessa. They were so kind to me that I loved being called auntie. So, my friend, this is the story of my first and only love until today."

— Very interesting! — Paulo obviously didn't know what to say.

— Sometimes I feel sad because it didn't work out with Thiago. If he had stayed in Brazil, only God knows how things would be today. All I know is that I never met anyone capable of provoking that same passion in me. You know something curious? When I was a child, my grandmother made me believe that not every thorn in the rosebush hurts your finger. Because Thiago was as sweet as a flower, I believed he was the thorn that would not hurt me. However, I was wrong. Or wasn't I?

— You live and learn.

— I agree! After all, life is like that, hard to understand. Whether I like it or not, I'm glad I had this experience of love at least once in my life.

— And who knows? There is a lot in this life we can still experience.

— Yes, it's possible — Vanessa said, hesitant and hopeful at the same time.

They were silent for a moment. The stars in the sky had gathered above the sea, and the brightness of these shining stars reflected on the surface of the ocean. Unexpectedly, a sense of serenity entered

Vanessa's core. This must have happened because she quickly remembered the two favorite characters from her grandmother Maria's stories. They were Marco and his master, François LePain. Grandma Maria told Vanessa that once, while these two men were walking in a deserted place, with no water or any signs of life, Marco was desperate. François LePain, who was not like any other master, realized the sadness of his servant and said, "O Marco, noble servant, know that the future is nothing but a box of good surprises." Marco was happy immediately. By the end of the journey, everything turned out fine.

At some point, Vanessa remembered that she had another appointment and said, "Oh my God! I forgot the party. I must leave now." As she got up quickly, she hugged her friend and ended up kissing him on his lips mistakenly. It appears that the kiss was by accident, and she apologized immediately.

— I am sorry, my friend. It was supposed to be a kiss on your cheek.

— I know. Don't worry! These things happen.

Paulo insisted on escorting her to a taxi. Thereafter, he also took a taxi and returned home. While he was sitting in the car, he kept thinking about the girl in the poem and Vanessa's kiss. The poem of the red rose came to him at Park Lage in an unusual way. The kiss was purely accidental. At least, that's what Vanessa said. Now Paulo was perplexed, trying, in vain, to understand the connection between all these events.

Arriving home, he entered the song *I'm Gonna Be* by The Proclaimers on YouTube and listened to it repeatedly. As he understood English, he ended up falling in love with the lyrics. Finally, the chorus was engraved in his spirit. Paulo went to bed, listening to this song in his mind.

But I would walk 500 miles
And I would walk 500 more
Just to be the man who walks a thousand miles
To fall down at your door
Da da da (da da da)
Da da da (da da da)
Da da da dun diddle un diddle un diddle uh da

Minutes later, Paulo fell asleep, dreaming of Vanessa. In his dream, they kissed. However, that kiss was not by mistake. The next day, he woke up even more confused with everything that was happening.

After thinking a little more about it, he realized that yearning for the future would not answer his questions about love. He had only one thing to do — let time heal the questions of his heart. And what would be the point of yearning for what was still to come? François LePain had already said that the future is a box of good surprises.

XIII
Grandma Maria's stories

When Vanessa was six, her parents moved from Rio to Goiânia because her mother had passed the public exams to become a judge in this city. Her father, who was already a successful lawyer, thought about establishing a second office there. He opened this branch near the Civic Square, not far from the Court of Justice building, located in the western part of the city. He was a labor lawyer, working with large companies.

Vanessa's parents had a well-regulated life, perfectly organized, sometimes even with a little paranoia, which was not good for their mental health. Maybe that's why they were both seeing a psychiatrist. It was clear that they had some issues to solve.

Since Vanessa's mother was a criminal judge, she and her husband were much more concerned about future events than the present. They always looked for the best way to deal with the ups and downs of their existence, and their lives were limited only to their jobs. They rarely stayed home and had no amusements. Besides being serious people, they took the greatest care with their commutes so as not to put themselves in danger. From time to time, they were informed of the homicides of another jurist who worked in criminal justice. They lived in constant fear of losing their lives — lives that consisted only of work.

Together with Vanessa, they lived in a gated community called Valley Village, in a large house worth more than three million reals, made entirely of wood. Valley Village is considered one of the most exclusive housing areas in the city, perhaps the most imposing. Inside this impressive development, adorned by abundant vegetation, there are several commercial and sports establishments, dozens of lakes, an equestrian club with specially trained employees, bistros with international cuisine, dry cleaners, supermarkets, and much more.

Sometimes monkeys, deer, foxes, capybaras, and other animals were seen around the yards of the houses in Valley Village. When Vanessa was a child, she liked to walk with a camera hanging from her neck, always prepared to record the moments when she came across these animals. Several times she found herself face to face with deer that stared at her with a penetrating look, or with monkeys that invaded the houses searching for food.

Unlike other children of the same age, Vanessa did not see her parents when she woke up in the morning. They were very busy, always dedicated to finding a better life for their daughter. When Vanessa complained about their absence, they said, "Honey, we do all this for you. When you grow up, you will understand, and you will thank us." Vanessa never understood her parents' reasoning. So, when she wasn't at school, she would walk alone through the spacious rooms of the wooden house, raised from the earth like a sunset-colored castle.

For many years, she wished her relationship with her parents was different. However, her parents never changed. She finally got used to their absence, even though they lived together. They left early in the morning and returned home late at night. Vanessa spent long hours in that luxurious house, with a large swimming pool and an impeccable leisure area. The truth is that she was not happy to be in that highly exclusive place. Very early in life, she realized that people's happiness is not always about wealth. Thus, she started not to care about outer appearances.

Besides missing her parents, she longed for something that was outside the boundaries of her home. She even thought that the solution to her sadness was waiting for her in the parks and lakes of the gated community. Unfortunately, even walking with her close friend Thiago around these places, she could not find the key to happiness. Inside, she had many questions. Unfortunately, neither her parents nor her neighbors could answer them. Nothing in that huge residence satisfied the emptiness that inhabited Vanessa's heart. She searched for the answer to her sadness but could not find it. However, while searching, she discovered something that cheered her up from time to time. It was nothing more than the beautiful singing of the birds, which calmed her heart every morning.

Once, while swimming in the pool, she saw an eagle flying over the house. Although she wasn't sure it was an eagle, she chose to believe it. The huge bird, free in the sky, was flying majestically. When she saw this, Vanessa was happy, with a feeling of freedom like that bird's. Unfortunately, since she rarely left that gated community, she soon realized she was not a free bird. She was a little bird trapped in a gilded cage. That's the way she grew up, with plenty of luxuries and little freedom.

At school, Vanessa did not have many friends. Her parents pressed her to be the best in her class, and this spirit of competition was not good for friendships. It was common for friendships to end when one's classmates got a better grade. Vanessa never wished evil on anyone. She just wanted to be the best in her class, as her colleagues did too. After all, what's wrong with wanting to be better than others? Anyway, Vanessa was too immature to know that being better than herself was much more valuable than being better than others.

Since Vanessa's parents were rarely at home, she felt invisible. They only saw her when they needed her to do something. And she almost never had anything to do but study and stay at home with her maid, just like a prisoner with her prison guard.

Dulce, the maid, didn't have much time to spend with Vanessa because the house was huge and taking care of it required significant effort. Even so, she was the only person who had more affinity with the young girl. She knew Vanessa more than Vanessa's own mother because she had taken care of her since they had moved to Goiania.

Vanessa learned almost nothing from her parents, since they never talked about anything but law, crime, and punishment. When they were not talking about these things, they locked themselves in their respective offices, sometimes to determine sentences, some other times to file petitions. Despite their busy schedules, they decided not to work on Sundays. But the truth is that her father spent hours watching the news, jumping from one channel to another, constantly looking for more information. Her mother spent the whole day resting on her refined bed. Although Sunday was the only day her parents stayed home, Vanessa only saw them when they had lunch and dinner.

Feeling an immense loneliness, she would sometimes sit in a corner of the courtyard, thinking about the past when they lived in Rio. At that time, her mother was studying for the examination to become a judge and, as usual, she did not pay much attention to her. Her father took care of his legal proceedings in his office during the day. At night, when he came home, he would only talk about legal cases and hearings, always complaining about the procedural deadlines. Vanessa, in silence, found her father's obsession with time unnecessary. In Vanessa's memories, her parents were always the same. The years added up, and they did not change anything in their routine. Once, when she was a child, she complained to her grandmother Maria about her parents' indifference.

The old woman told her, "When you live in just one way, it is very difficult to see the infinite possibilities that life offers you. You just need to learn to be better than your parents when you grow up."

Now Vanessa, in her residence in Goiânia, found herself missing her earlier life. The past pleased her more than the present, as she remembered the stories Grandma Maria had told her. Most of them dealt with the adventures of Marco and his master, François LePain. She seemed to know everything about those two men. The only thing she did not know was how they had met. One day, Vanessa asked her grandmother, "Grandma, how did Marco and his master François LePain meet?"

— Marco was a poor Spaniard, and François LePain, a wealthy Frenchman. The two met long before they came into this world. They were friends before France and Spain existed. But my dear, what's the use of trying to know where they came from or where they were going? — she stopped for a moment. — What we need to know about these two men is that they walked the world and taught people like me the most important thing in life.

— What? — Vanessa asked immediately.

Her grandmother answered gently.

— The river flowed slowly but tirelessly. The dark sky, full of shining stars, sparkled like a diamond. Marco was admiring the silent dance of the current when his master François LePain said, "Life is full of infinite things. However, of all these, only one really matters — Love. It is at the beginning and at the end of all existence — Maria took her granddaughter's hand. — Love is all that is needed in this life, my dear.

— I get it, grandma.

When Vanessa and her parents lived in Rio, she visited her grandmother on weekends, and they talked for hours. Vanessa spent a good part of her childhood listening to the stories about Marco and his master, François LePain. Now she lived in a house full of opulence. There, she missed her grandmother, who had died a year earlier and who had given her so much affection and love.

XIV
Serving

Before Vanessa started studying at Law School, she thought she would make good and sincere friends during the course. However, soon after starting her studies, she realized that most of her colleagues were more concerned with the appearance of things than with the sincerity of their words. In the faculty corridors, it was very common to come across a student wanting to prove that he knew more than the others. Most of the teachers did the same too. Through their attitude, they taught students by example.

Fortunately, Vanessa had classes with three special teachers. They talked a lot about love, so almost nobody attended their classes. Since most students cared more about the law than love, they found these classes boring.

In the first term of the program, Vanessa's colleagues liked to speak about naturalism and positivism. As time went by, the conversations began to follow two opposite directions, where the students never reached a consensus. Friendships were held hostage to different currents of thought. As for the university in general, it should be noted that not all students could accept this environment of endless friction. Vanessa was one of them and felt like a princess outside her castle. Once again, she felt out of place, misunderstood by those around her. She, occasionally, watched the academic debates through which her colleagues sought the balance between the extremes. The only problem they always found in this task was that the balance of justice always hung to one side. François LePain had already told his disciple Marco, "The balance of justice is like a small flame. It wavers before the wind when the judge's heart trembles before truth."

In the end, Vanessa was convinced that five years of her life had been squandered in that university, all those years studying what was already in the books. Was she right or not? Either way, she found those years very long and sad. She felt surrounded by colleagues who had nothing to share with her. They, however, were pleased to be taking a course that evoked dignity.

Vanessa's colleagues were not very different from her parents. She thought that this sad reality was not her colleagues' or her parents' fault. This is because people in general have almost nothing to share with each other. Once she even thought it was the universe's fault, but finally, she thought, "It is only for God to reveal whose fault it is because men believe it is not theirs."

Since in life there are always two sides to the same coin, it is important to remember that throughout the program, along with her dissatisfaction, Vanessa occasionally had fun, especially with one of her colleagues. His name was Erico, but everyone called him Mister Black. He had earned this nickname because he always wore a black suit, rain or shine. Despite the heat, he was always wearing a business suit. Sometimes it was thirty-five degrees, and the heat burned like fire on his skin, but his belief that a good lawyer should always wear a suit made Mister Black's heart beat with more joy. From time to time, the black tie hanging from his neck nearly suffocated him. And even though he found it difficult to breathe, Mister Black continued firmly and resolutely with his eloquent debates, which dealt with issues of Law. In his intimidating speeches, he liked to use far-fetched words and gestured like a happy monkey. Even without understanding anything Mister Black said, Vanessa learned to like him because each of his lines was like a very entertaining play.

Soon after graduating, Vanessa got a commissioned position in a Judge's office in the Court of Justice. She became an aide to an appellate court judge and worked there for seven years. During that time, she had a boyfriend named Luis. They met in the workplace. Two days after meeting, they started dating. After six years of dating, Vanessa began to question her boyfriend about getting married. In her heart, she did not love him, but she thought marriage would make her a fulfilled woman. However, he needed some more time.

— Time for what? — she asked her boyfriend one night.

Luis pretended he did not hear and went back to sleep. The next day, she asked the same question.

— I want some more time to have a better standard of living, — Luis answered coldly.

— What better standard of living? — Vanessa asked, indignant.

Vanessa asked these questions because Luis was already a brilliant and successful lawyer. He was one of those lawyers who liked to show off in designer suits. The fact that he did not want to decide triggered the end of their relationship. A few months after the breakup, Luis married another girl, who also placed a lot of attention on her appearance and way of dressing. Vanessa was invited to the wedding ceremony. During the celebration, she realized that Luis was happy, with happiness he had never shown when they were together. Surprisingly, she was not sad to realize this. On the contrary, she forgot the past and opened her heart to receive what was to come.

Vanessa, single again, began to travel the world, visiting more than fifteen countries. Her first trip was very significant for her. She went to South Africa to learn about the wild kingdom. Until then, she thought there were only safaris in Africa. But it wasn't her fault because the media had taken care of teaching her that. In South Africa, everything was different from what she expected. With much enthusiasm, she set foot in Tambo International Airport, one of the two international airports, a cozy, neighborhood-wide establishment in Johannesburg. In the city, everything was very well maintained, with good roads, monuments, and beautiful buildings. In fact, Johannesburg is a metropolitan city, and Vanessa needed to see that for herself. Her surprise was even greater when she came across an economic reality drastically different from what appeared in the newspapers. It is no accident that many consider this city The City of Gold.

As a tourist in South Africa, Vanessa did not see anyone in extreme poverty. Maybe because she only walked through the most affluent parts of the city. She knew that poverty, although found in different degrees, exists everywhere in the world. However, she realized that on the African continent there is not only misery and poverty. There is also wealth and joy. During her stay in South Africa, she fell in love with the welcoming people, who treated her with great love and respect. She also noticed that in this country, animals do not go about in the streets, attacking and devouring people. So Vanessa had to visit a national park to go on a safari. It was a unique experience, the discovery of another reality, which she enjoyed greatly.

After South Africa, she went to Tunisia, and there, in the city of Tunis, she met a Brazilian couple who were on their honeymoon. They told her that they had chosen this destination to honor the memory of her husband's great-grandparents. They were two French citizens who had fled Hitler's invasion during World War II. They met in that country and got married soon afterward. A few years after their fortuitous marriage, they moved to Southern Brazil. Vanessa loved hearing this story. When she left Tunis, she went to Egypt to see the great pyramids of Giza. On the African continent, she also passed through Algeria and Morocco.

Getting to know a part of Africa was a liberating experience, as she had grown up believing everything people said about that continent. Now she realized that it is always good to have your own experiences instead of trusting other opinions.

After this first travel experience, Vanessa became addicted to the idea of meeting new people and new cultures. This way, she worked all year round, and when she took a vacation, she immediately packed her bags and traveled through several countries. She became a well-traveled person.

The crazy or the ordinary adventures she experienced in her travels had the effect of inhibiting the feeling of loneliness that plagued her. All her life, she had always felt lonely until she began to travel, but unfortunately in life, nothing lasts forever. Over time, being an outsider in foreign lands no longer satisfied her. Nothing really calmed her heart until she went to the Bahamas, where she liked the way the locals served and treated foreigners. At the time, she had an insight into her inner dissatisfaction and thought, "What I am seeking is service." This did not mean that she did not serve through her work as a legal advisor. The truth is that she wanted to serve in a gentler and lighter environment, where she could have more direct contact with people.

After returning from that trip, some months passed before she decided what she had to do to feel happy. Finally, she stopped working at the Court of Justice and moved back to Rio, her hometown, where she started her own business — Café Sorriso.

XV
Don Juan of Lisbon

One year after getting to know a bit of Africa, Vanessa decided to visit Europe, more precisely Portugal. There she was, in her beautiful dress, walking down the narrow streets of Lisbon, up and down stairs, going from one place to another, enjoying the sights. She was happy on the streets of Lisbon, and that was what mattered most to her. She looked perfect in those simple but elegant clothes. An unparalleled sensitivity was concealed within her gaze. She displayed a sweetness in her way of being, and sometimes a smile at the corners of her lips.

When she went out at night, she felt she attracted many looks. Some men approached her, thinking that she might be an easy girl. Right at the beginning, she would say she was a legal advisor in Brazil, and they would disappear in the same way they had appeared. As a loving person, she conquered the heart of Lisbon little by little, and thus made friends with some people in the city. Nobody could explain, herself included, the joy that emanated from her. Sometimes she associated her enthusiasm for life with the warm climate in Brazil.

While Vanessa was strolling in Lisbon, she admired the beauties the city offers to tourists. It is a pretty city, raised from the earth like a princess. Everything about it was fascinating — the buildings, the streets, the trees, and the people. In the morning, the sun's rays hit the city, leaving it radiant like a fairy. In short, Lisbon was simply magnificent. On her walking tours, Vanessa realized that she had fallen in love with the city in a very short time.

One night, while she was sitting in a bar, she noticed some men wanting to approach her. She was not very comfortable with this, but she knew that not all men are the same. In one of her grandmother Maria's stories, François LePain said to his servant Marco, "Learn not to judge the son by his father's actions because men are not always the same."

In the second week of her stay in Lisbon, she met Ronaldo. He was certainly not an ordinary man. Almost every night, Ronaldo went out looking for a female company. One night, Vanessa was in a bar when, Ronaldo appeared. He was tall, dark, and elegant.

— Bonsoir, Madame. Comment-allez vous?

Vanessa knew only enough to say that she didn't speak French. She then answered, smiling.

— Bonsoir, Monsieur. Je ne parle pas français.

They both smiled. She realized that Ronaldo was joking. He continued the conversation in Portuguese.

— Are you Brazilian?

— Yes, I am. What about you? Are you the Frenchman of Lisbon? She asked ironically.

— I am a Portuguese who speaks French in Lisbon — he said, smiling.

While they were talking, Vanessa noticed that Ronaldo's breath was minty, which showed that he didn't smoke or drink. She then became more engaged in the conversation. Ronaldo liked soccer, and Vanessa loved Ronaldo, the Phenomenon. That's how they started talking about which Ronaldo was the best in the world — Cristiano Ronaldo from Portugal or Ronaldo from Brazil. It was a lively discussion, and Vanessa ended up agreeing that Cristiano Ronaldo was the best because he rarely got hurt.

— I agree with you, just because Cristiano Ronaldo has never hurt his knee — she said to close off the choice of the best Ronaldo in the world.

When the waiter asked Ronaldo what he wanted, he answered, "A bottle of water, please."

Vanessa smiled and ordered the same thing. She liked polite men, and Ronaldo was very polite. So, right after they started the conversation, he did not take long to win her over. At least, that is what he thought. Vanessa learned a lot about Ronaldo that night. There was just one thing she did not know about him. She did not know that he went to bars every night and flirted with every woman he met. He often spoke French to them, and they loved his charm. He told them he had learned French in Paris, La Ville Lumière. He also said that in Paris, love is king and subject at the same time, and it was everywhere, in every gaze. He told them that in Paris, love conquered the hearts of all without having to subdue them. He talked about boat rides along the Seine. He told them about his romantic adventures in the parks, gardens, and museums of Paris. And finally, he listed the restaurants famous for French gastronomy. Thus, he conquered the hearts of unknown women who were passing through Lisbon.

The Paris flirtation was repeated with Vanessa, and she listened with enthusiasm and curiosity. In his heart, Ronaldo was happy because he thought he was conquering this woman from Rio. Sometimes he would smile at her, and she would smile back. At that moment, they were navigators, and passion was their sea.

While talking to Vanessa, Ronaldo was elegant, like a noble gentleman before a princess. However, he was also a born Don Juan. He liked women, but never took them seriously. He was always flirting, dividing himself among the romances of the nights in Lisbon. This was his dark and romantic side at the same time.

On the other hand, Vanessa looked at him with desire and found the idea of a passing romance interesting. Since she had broken up with Luis, she had not had any relationships. "A romance! Why not? I'm single, and so is he," she thought and carried on with the conversation. She did not want anything serious. So she offered her heart to Ronaldo that night.

Vanessa's beautiful face conquered Ronaldo entirely. The way she looked at him, as dangerous as an arrow, hit him, and he desired her as he desired all women. He did not know that Vanessa was no ordinary woman. From conversation to conversation, the love between them was consummated. Sometimes they did not understand each other very well because Ronaldo spoke with a strong Portuguese accent. However, that was no obstacle to their physical closeness. Besides, Ronaldo was a master at love with strangers. Vanessa, on the other hand, was only enjoying having a one-time adventure. After making love, they slept in peace, embracing each other. The next day, Ronaldo surprised himself when he did something he had never done before — he spent the day with the stranger. More surprising still, he tried to speak Portuguese with a Brazilian accent. He said, "Vanessa, would you like to come to Paris with me?" Vanessa was delighted and thought, "Paris? Wow, how romantic!" Then she answered, "Yes, I would like that very much."

Two days later, they went to Paris, where they went sightseeing and spent a lot of time together. One morning, while Vanessa was still sleeping, Ronaldo watched her for several minutes. He had already fallen in love. Deep in his heart, he knew she was just enjoying this romance in the present moment.

At some time, he took his cell phone and typed "Vanessa". He was curious to know the origin of that name. He found on Google that Vanessa was the name of a butterfly. However, he was not satisfied with that and searched the Internet until he found a French

Café called "Vanessa". After Vanessa woke up, Ronaldo took her to this café. At the entrance, there was a framed poem in French.

D'une romance à l'autre,
Elle est une passionnée.
D'un pays à l'autre,
Elle est une romantique.
Elle vole, elle voyage,
Avec le sac à dos.
Et l'amour toujours à ses côtés.

— Ronaldo, could you please translate it for me? — said Vanessa.

— Sure!

Ronaldo read the poem to Vanessa.

From one romance to another,
She is passionate.
From one country to another,
She is romantic.
She flies, she travels,
With a pack on her back.
And love always at her side.

At that moment, he realized that the romance with Vanessa had no future, and that she would probably never come to Lisbon again. For the first time, he felt sad in the middle of an affair. And this, in fact, was the best and the most intense of all the affairs he had experienced until then. For years, he had played with women's hearts, loving them only for one night, and most of them fell in love with him. To all these women, he would say, "I am not made to love. I like dating. It's something I can't change."

The only problem with Vanessa is that she never talked about love nor about passion. She talked about many things, but never about Ronaldo's charm and the possibility of one day returning to

Lisbon. Maybe it was because for her, it was nothing more than a pleasant experience. Ronaldo, on the other hand, was very much in love with her. He felt hurt because she did not return his passion. But what could he do? Vanessa didn't even know she was hurting him. She was there just enjoying her trip and loving Europe as much as she could. At a certain moment, while they were walking in Paris, Ronaldo asked her, "Vanessa, what do you think of me?"

— You're very nice, and you have good vibes.

Although Ronaldo was disappointed and saddened by her answer, he didn't show it. Deep down, he wanted her to find him handsome and fascinating. But things in life don't always happen as we wish. And Vanessa didn't mean to harm anyone. She was just enjoying her trip. So, she returned to Brazil thrilled, unaware that she had broken someone's heart.

Ronaldo, on the other hand, returned to Lisbon disheartened. By thinking a lot about Vanessa, he ended up unlocking her secret, a secret that perhaps even she herself didn't know —Vanessa was a world traveler, hard to get to know, hard to conquer. However, it was effortless to love her and to fall in love with her. She walked the roads of the Earth, always following the flow of life, going where the wind took her, not worrying about what might happen. She simply enjoyed the present moment.

After she left, Ronaldo kept thinking about his relationship with Vanessa. At one point, he put himself in the place of the women who had fallen in love with him. He realized, then, that he had not always acted in the best way with them. He had treated them without valuing them, without honoring their love. From then on, despite continuing to be elegant and gentlemanly with women, Ronaldo decided to love one woman at a time and did not mind waiting for the right one as long as it took.

At night, in Lisbon, instead of going to bars, he would stay at home, read a little and write love poems. As time went by, he stopped being the Don Juan of Lisbon and became the greatest romantic poet in town. Once, while giving a lecture on love, he told his listeners, "Every woman is a queen and should be treated as such."

If we dwell in spirit, or Soul, we are living in happiness, for Soul is a happy entity.
Paul Twitchell

XVI
Contemplation

Before meeting with Paulo, Karina remembered when she was looking for continuity in her spiritual practices. She had spent time at the Findhorn Ecovillage in Scotland and in Auroville, in India. They were exceptional places, where she thought she could find what she was looking for. First, she spent fifteen days in Findhorn. Hundreds of people were living in this community, harmonizing with nature. Their members organized activities with a holistic aspect.

Although Karina greatly enjoyed this experience, she received an inner guidance not to stay there. Thereafter, she decided to spend some time in Auroville, India. It is a village that embodies the idea that men and women from all over the world can share a life of peace and happiness, no matter the politics, nationality, or belief.

She really enjoyed the spiritual experience she had in these two places, but she felt in her heart that life there was not for her. So she went back to Rio. Some time later, she realized she needed to meet a need for individuality in her journey of self-knowledge. That's why living in a community was not the answer to what she was seeking.

After remembering all this, Karina went to meet Paulo at the Christ the Redeemer, which is in the Tijuca National Park, majestically built on the summit of Corcovado hill. Christ the Redeemer opens His arms to receive men as they are, without discrimination or preference. Thus, he teaches men that there is nothing more beautiful than love in this life.

Karina and Paulo had the feeling that God was present in everything around them. The sun was shining in the clear sky, and the city spread itself below the emblematic statue of Jesus Christ. Divided between nature and modernity, Rio showed itself as the most beautiful city in the world.

While Paulo, with his thoughtful gaze, was admiring the imposing city in which he was born, he remembered when he was a child. At that time, he loved going to the Christ, but in fact went there very rarely. His father never agreed with this representation of the Messiah. He thought that the son of God was omnipotent and could not be limited to a statue.

Now, Paulo was no longer that disciplined boy who believed in ready-made religious doctrines. As an adult, he was at a critical moment in his life. He had reached a point where he no longer knew what to believe. However, faith was not lost in his heart. He just did not know what direction to take.

Karina started the conversation:

— What about your parents? Are they well?

— I just have my father. My mother has already died.

— I'm sorry!

— That's all right!

— Is your father well?

— I think so. The truth is that we don't talk very often.

— What happened? Would you like to talk about it?

— I just think he and I have different points of view.

— If you want to talk, go ahead.

— I don't know if I should talk about it.

— You can if you think it will help you.

— I think it will.

— I'm glad! — said Karina.

Paulo began speaking.

— My father is a pastor who has a good heart. We had a disagreement when my mother passed away. I think I should tell you a little about my mother, and then you will understand the story better.

— All right. Please go ahead.

— When my mother was younger, she dreamed of working in the health area. However, life determined otherwise. It turns out that she had a talent for hairdressing, and suddenly, she decided to work in that field, and opened a beauty salon. The problem began in my childhood. When I was growing up, my mother wanted me to be a doctor to realize her frustrated dream. Unfortunately, I followed another path, and from that point on, my relationship with her and my father began to deteriorate. Even when she was on her deathbed at the hospital, she didn't forgive me for following my own will. The last day I saw her, she was bedridden. She was in a terminal stage of cancer and had lost a lot of weight. I was sorry, seeing her so weak in that hospital bed. I couldn't do anything to help her. She had always been a strong woman, and it was a shock to see her with no strength at all. She and I were talking when I started to cry. There was no way to be strong seeing her suffering so much. She told me she was happy with her imminent departure. But it was hard to accept when she whispered that she would like to have been treated by her son. I regretted not doing what she had wanted, and I didn't feel worthy of her. I didn't have the courage to visit her again until she passed away. I grew up admiring her. She was a strong woman, a heroic mother, a person who inspired me in everything I did. I couldn't handle the situation when I realized she wasn't proud of me when she died. After she passed away, I distanced myself from my father too. He complained a lot about the fact that I didn't visit her in those difficult moments. It was a very delicate situation, and it's hard to talk about it. I regret having acted that way. However, today, almost four years after she passed away, I can understand my mother's reasons. Parents usually put their dreams on their children's shoulders.

— Haven't you ever thought of being a doctor, as your mother wished?

— No, never. The truth is that I was a sickly child. I spent so much time in hospital that I started to hate everything related to medicine. Besides, the other great dilemma of my life was that, deep down, I did not know what job I really wanted to do. I have always wondered what I wanted from life, and what it wanted from me. However, I've never gotten an answer. Today, at forty-eight, after being jobless for over two years, I still don't know what to do.

Karina interrupted Paulo and asked, "How do you support yourself?"

— Thank God, I don't have to worry about money. My salary was very high when I was working, so I was able to save a lot of money at that time. Besides, I spend very little. My ex-wife kept our apartment in Ipanema after the divorce, and now I live in a small apartment in Copacabana.

— Have you ever tried to clear the air with your father?

— It would be no use. He is just like my late mother, he never listens. It's been over three years since we had a good conversation. He still resents me.

— I can imagine how difficult the loss of your mother was for both of you. But I believe a sincere conversation will be able to mitigate and, who knows, even solve this conflicted situation. As for your mother, you could try to forgive her, and more importantly, forgive yourself. After all, it seems that everything she did was to protect you.

— I find it very difficult to talk to my father about all this. Because he is a pastor, he thinks he is the custodian of God's words and believes he is always right. So I am not sure how he will react.

— Only God knows about such things! But you must do your part. He may surprise you.

— True. But what can one do when dealing with a person who doesn't listen?

— Usually, when I realize that someone doesn't like to listen, I simply listen to that person and keep my words in my heart. Sometimes, we make much more of the conversation by being silent.

They smiled. Then Paulo put his hand on his forehead and thought a little. Perplexed, he asked Karina, "Speaking of the dilemmas of life, what do you do when doubts torment you?"

— I do a spiritual exercise called "contemplation".

— Just that?

— Yes — Karina answered succinctly, smiling all the time.

— Hmm! — Paulo frowned. — Is it that simple?

— Yes, it is.

— Can you please explain a little more how you do "contemplation?"

— Sure! Contemplation is basically a spiritual practice that helps us go to our inner temple. That way, you get to know yourself little by little as you contemplate. It is a way for you to meet yourself while living here on Earth, a way to experience happiness from the inside out. In this way, we can find peace regardless of the circumstances of life, whether positive or negative.

— When you talk about the inner temple, are you talking about the Soul?

— That's right!

— It's interesting to realize that Socrates had already pondered this millennia ago.

— True. He said, "Know thyself and you shall know the universe and the Gods."

— When I think about this affirmation by Socrates, the same question always arises, a riddle difficult to decipher.

— What is the question?

— What seems to be lacking to make us feel happy is completeness, right?

— Yes, that's right.

— My question about happiness is that if we really have everything within us, if the Soul is already complete, why then do we project our fullness onto things or people?

— Maybe the problem with the pursuit of happiness is that we spend too much energy, time, and money, and in the end, nothing satisfies us. On the other hand, I believe that if you seek spiritual freedom, I mean, if you touch the fullness within yourself daily, you won't depend on a happiness based on external conditions.

— Would that be going to the inner temple?

— Exactly!

— How interesting! There was a time when I practiced meditation. I was able to silence my mind, but I can't tell if I have ever been to my inner temple. Who knows? Perhaps I have, but unconsciously.

— Well, in terms of going to the inner temple, contemplation is a gentler and at the same time more active way than meditation. You know, without conflicting with the mind, not trying to force it to silence itself, just letting thoughts flow like the river of life. Sometimes they disappear. Some other times, they make themselves present, becoming more and more relevant to the questions of the moment.

— Could I contemplate singing a mantra?

— Yes. You can.

— I see that many people like to sing OM. Do you know any other mantra that has a similar vibration?

— Yes, I do. Besides OM, I also sing HU. I realize that the vibration of HU is a little more subtle. But I believe that each person prefers a certain mantra.

— Karina, have you ever had an insight during your contemplation? I mean, a creative idea, an answer to a question or a solution to any problem in life?

— Yes, I have. In fact, this has happened several times. But insights can come at any moment of the day apart from the contemplation, sometimes before going to sleep, in your dreams or when you are in silence. I believe that if you are open, you will always be in communication with the universe.

Paulo said happily, "Now, I clearly understand how life can be blessed when one knows how to listen to the universe and work with it."

— True! After all, everything depends on us. That's why I like to think that life is simple.

Paulo agreed and said, "Karina, you have such a wise way of seeing life! I am deeply grateful that I can learn from you."

— I am happy to talk about life! — Karina said with a look full of satisfaction.

From the top of Corcovado hill, Paulo looked down to the neighborhoods below, and the view of the city amazed him. He then closed his eyes and instantly felt a wave of peace conquering his core. At that moment, he had the feeling that the universe and he formed a single entity. He breathed the soft air and said, "I think I should visit my father immediately. I want to talk to him about my feelings."

Karina asked him, "Shouldn't you let him know beforehand?"

— It's not necessary. He spends the whole day at home since he retired from the church.

As they walked down from the Christ, Paulo found that it was much easier to go down than up. Then he thought about his own life. It had taken many years to build a decent life, and suddenly, from one day to the next, he had lost everything. But now he knew that happiness in life does not depend on external things.

As she left, Karina said, "Good luck with your father!"

— Thank you, Karina!

And they went their separate ways.

XVII
The way

Diego's death was a reality that Paulo took time to accept. He loved his cousin very much, and this loss in some way also contributed to his estrangement from his father. At that time, Paulo was trying in vain to understand God's justice. He wondered how Diego could have died in the prime of life.

Gabriel, his father, was not very helpful when Paulo was trying to find an answer. He recited Bible verses to explain everything that happened in life. Paulo got to the point where he couldn't stand listening to his father's sermons anymore and would leave the house to play soccer with his friends in the neighborhood. At that time, only soccer could cheer Paulo up. He played each match as if it were his last. He complained a lot when his team lost. He took soccer so seriously that nobody wanted him to be part of their team.

Paulo skipped church services to play soccer, and his father would become embarrassed in front of his congregation. Gabriel once said to his son, "You should not be out on the street with people who don't attend church." It was remarkable how different Paulo was from his father. Every so often, he acted as if he were not a pastor's son.

Years later, when Paulo lost his job, his father, instead of supporting him, tried to blame him. He said he had offered him the hand of God, but he preferred to follow the path of perdition. Paulo stopped counting how many times his father had told him, "Don't you think it's better to save lives than to work in finance?" He could never accept his son's choice to be an economist.

Going back in time, the sorrow in Paulo's heart toward his father had deep roots. One night, he asked his father about the meaning of life. He couldn't answer and just said, "Everything in life happens by Divine Grace." In fact, he always evoked Divine Grace to answer his son's questions, as if this was a formula for all kinds of questions. Paulo then began to doubt his father. He also felt disappointed because he thought a pastor must have the right answer for every situation in life.

"What's the use of all this effort to find happiness in life when you come to Earth and leave with nothing?" That was one of the many questions Paulo carried with him everywhere he went. Now, in the present moment, he decided to visit his father after having spoken with Karina. He went to the house where he grew up, not far from Botafogo Beach. The last time he had talked to his father was after his mother's death, more than three years earlier.

— Good afternoon, Dad!

— Good afternoon, my son!

— Is everything okay with you?

— Yes, it is. What about with you, my son?

— Everything is okay as well.

They were silent, and the atmosphere began to weigh on them. Gabriel did not seem enthusiastic about his son's visit. He knew that there are wounds that time does not heal. The wound, although not visible to the naked eye, is hidden in the heart. Sometimes it only takes warm words to heal the wounded person's heart and to dispel the resentment. As Karina said to Paulo, a sincere conversation is capable of alleviating and, who knows, even resolving a conflict.

Gabriel finally broke the silence:

— Why did you stop visiting her?

— Visiting who?

— Your mother.

— The last time I went to see her at the hospital, she told me she would like me to be the doctor who treated her. I realized that she had not forgiven me for choosing another profession. So I thought I was not worthy of her, and I didn't go back to the hospital anymore.

— You know very well how your mother was. She was always a stubborn person, but that doesn't mean she didn't love you.

— That's true. I understand her now.

— You seem wiser. What's happening to you?

— I think we learn about ourselves over the years. Today, I know I hurt you very much, and I apologize from the bottom of my heart.

— I suffered a lot with the loss of your mother, but I suffered even more when you walked away from me. Right now, I am delighted to heal the wounds of the past. Come here! Give me a hug!

— I'm happy as well, Dad.

They hugged, with their faces full of tears of forgiveness. Then Paulo said, "The maid told me that you don't go to church very often now."

— It's true! After retiring, I spent months at home, and this helped me understand an important thing.

— What is that?

— My son, I have concluded that within us there is everything we need in life. The kingdom of God is not in any specific cult or temple. It is in the heart of every being. And the only way to reach the Holy Father is Love.

Paulo listened in wonder to his father talking about the path that leads to God, very similar to what Karina had said when they were standing next to the Christ. They both spoke about going to the inner temple. For the first time in his life, his father told him something that would help him solve one of his great dilemmas. He smiled at his father, as he experienced complete joy. Like a child who had long been thirsty for the word of God, he asked, "Dad, how can one find Love in everyday life?"

— It's simple, my son. In the Bible, in Matthew 22:37-39, we find, "Jesus replied: You shall love the Lord your God with all your heart and with all your soul and with all your mind. 38. This is the first and greatest commandment. 39. And the second is like it: Love your neighbor as yourself."

That day, Paulo and Gabriel surrendered to forgiveness. They smiled at each other again. In harmony, father and son were reconciled to become one thing — Love.

XVIII
Connecting diamonds

Today, Paulo awoke serene. He knew now that his father had never stopped loving him. Soon after waking up, he answered his children's messages over WhatsApp and sent a "Hi" to Karina.

[Hi, Karina, how are you?]

[I'm fine, and you?]

[I'm fine too!]

[Did everything go well with your father?] — Karina's message said.

[Yes, we are fine now. Thanks for suggesting that I talk to him.

[I'm glad to hear that]

[I've just remembered what you told me about contemplation in our last conversation. What do you think about meeting at the Botanical Garden for you to tell me more about this subject? Whichever day works for you.]

[We can meet there tomorrow at 9:00 a.m. if you like.]

[That works for me.]

[See you tomorrow.]

[See you.]

Karina found his suggestion excellent because she could do two things she liked very much — go for a walk and share what she knew about the Spiritual Freedom. It's worth pointing out that she did not talk to everyone about her spiritual achievements. It's something she only did with people who wanted to know about it.

"If I can find peace in myself, why not share it with others?" was Karina's thinking. Besides, she had very positive energy, and people wanted to know where it came from. Once, one of her friends looked at her and said, "You are always happy. How do you do that?" To which she replied, "I like to think that life is simple and beautiful." In fact, she had a code of conduct for dealing with her issues. This internal law consisted of never telling people the negative experiences of her personal life. This explanation did not make much sense to her friend because talking about his difficulties was what he knew best.

In this way, despite having problems like everyone else, Karina was always happy. She practiced the laws of silence and contentment, keeping her suffering to herself and offering her ears to those who really needed to get something off their chest or cry out their agonies. When you live like this, life can only be a fascinating and satisfying experience.

After exchanging messages with Karina, Paulo got up, made his bed, and had breakfast. Then he went for a walk along the beach. He changed a lot since he had met Karina, adding new habits to his daily life. Now he knew that body and spirit are one and the same, and for them to work properly, they must be coordinated in a harmonious way. Ulysses, a friend of Paulo's, a health lover, who was well known for taking such good care of his body, had already told him that every balanced body shelters a free and serene spirit. After the walk, the rest of the day went normally. When night came, Paulo slept well, and the next day he went to meet Karina. She was the first to arrive and was already waiting at the entrance to the Botanical Garden. After greeting each other, Karina and Paulo began to walk along a palm tree lane. She wanted to show him a palm tree that had been planted exactly on the day one of her brothers was born. She remembered always looking for this palm tree when she went with her parents and brothers to the Botanical Garden. Paulo loved to see the palm tree and said, "How interesting that you could follow the growth of the palm tree and your brother as the years went by."

— True! It was a good experience to see how humans and plants grow. Today, my brother is an adult, and the palm tree is very high.

— Karina, you once told me about how Contemplation works. Could you please tell me about how you discovered this practice?

— Sure! But it's quite a long story.

— We have all the time in the world — Paulo said with an ironic but amused look.

They both laughed because it was the same sentence Karina had said to him the day they met. She began to speak, while Paulo listened attentively.

— You know, in 1976, I was working as a flight attendant for a German airline. It was an interesting period of my life, a little tiring, but fascinating. I took this job to fill a void that I felt in my chest. It was a deep dissatisfaction that I had carried with me since my childhood. Thus, I thought that being a stewardess could cheer my heart, but I was wrong. As time went by, I realized I had to find something else to achieve the peace I desired. So, I took a course of meditation. They taught me how to go to my inner temple. When I had my first experience of going to the inner temple, I realized that this was what I had been seeking all my life. This practice gave me a feeling of relaxation, making me feel lighter and happier. This made me appreciate the good side of life. As I had an inner spiritual communion, I was increasingly able to accept the nature of the things in a physical world.

"The discovery of this spiritual practice was a significant step for me. But as time went by, the meditation group began putting their attention on some other aspects of spirituality. They started getting into levitation, a psychic practice, and that didn't interest me at all. Then I found a group from Rio created by a Frenchman named Pierre, who dealt mainly with transpersonal psychology. He lived in Belo Horizonte and coordinated groups in Rio and in Recife as well. I began to take part in the activities of this group and met many people who taught interesting courses, including some Tibetan monks. One day, I received a phone call from them inviting me to a talk given by a German woman who lived in Belo Horizonte. She lived in the same gated community as Pierre, and through him, she had access to invite all the people in the group. The lecture was about a path called Spiritual Freedom. I had heard of this group many years before. This had happened when I was still a stewardess. At that time, I had a co-worker named Monika, who also practiced meditation, and we always exchanged ideas about spirituality. That day, on a stopover of a few days in Dakar, we were sitting on the beach, contemplating the beauty of the sea, when suddenly she asked me if I had ever heard of the Spiritual Freedom. As I hadn't, she told me a few things, including that they always have a living Master at the head of the group. It turns out that, at that time, Monika shared her apartment with another stewardess. One night, she decided to go to the kitchen for some water. The next day, her roommate asked her, 'Monika, did you go to the kitchen for a glass of water last night?' 'Yes, I did! How do you know that?', Monika asked immediately. 'I was outside my body,' answered her friend with a smile. Suspicious, Monika asked me, 'Karina, don't you think this story is strange?' Amazed by all this, I didn't even know what to say, and I added, 'I agree! It's strange indeed.' The further information Monika gave me was that at the Spiritual Freedom they say that the Soul receives a body to have experiences in the school of life.

"When I stopped to think about it, I realized that it wasn't an absurd conception to see the Soul that way. So, when I got the invitation to attend the lecture, I quickly remembered the conversation on the beach in Dakar. At first, I imagined that this new experience could meet my expectations, but I needed to see it with my eyes. That's how I attended the lecture.

"In her presentation, Ingrid, the German woman, spoke a lot about the Spiritual Masters and the importance of being guided by those who have already progressed further in spirituality. When one lives on earth, the challenges are endless, and the lessons are many. After all, life is a school. How to progress spiritually without a Master to show the way? Wouldn't it be easier to tame fear when you learn from those who have already overcome it? Of course, it would! Ingrid also pointed out that the true Masters only show the way, thus allowing the students in the school of life to progress with their own feet. I listened carefully to Ingrid's talk on the subject, but I left the meeting with the feeling that I wasn't worthy of those teachings. I felt they were too advanced for me. When I got home, I went to sleep, and the next day I did my meditation as soon as I woke up. The inner voice, which I call my Inner Master, said, 'Look for that woman from yesterday's lecture.' I had already learned to listen to that inner voice and never doubted it. I then decided to talk to Ingrid. Knowing in which hotel she was staying, I called her, saying that I had been at the lecture the day before. She didn't take long to ask, 'Have you had breakfast yet?' I answered, 'Not yet.' And she continued, 'Why don't you come and have breakfast with me here at the hotel restaurant? We can talk and get to know each other better.' I agreed directly.

"During our conversation, I learned that she had also practiced meditation before. So, we had something in common. We talked a lot, and it turned out to be a nice chat, an interesting exchange of experiences. That day, I learned many new things, like the difference between Meditation and Contemplation. Contemplation is a much more active way of going to the inner temple. At the end of the dialogue, I thought, 'Maybe this way is for me. Why not try it?' When we said goodbye, Ingrid said that she would return to Rio in two months. Instantly, the Inner Master suggested that I invite her. Then I said immediately, 'If you like, you can stay at my house. I live with my parents, and we have a guest room.' Ingrid returned to Rio to give some other lectures in the months following, and as time went by, we became good friends. Once, after a talk, Ingrid said to me, 'You are so patient! You listen to the same thing several times and never get tired.' I answered that I liked to hear what she said.' When I went to her last lecture, a woman who was sitting next to me said, 'I think I will sign up for this spiritual path.' I listened to the Inner Master and said, 'Good idea! I think I'll sign up too.' Many things have happened in my life in this way. Someone next to me would decide to do something, and it was as if the universe were suggesting that I do the same. Two months after our enrollment at Spiritual Freedom, this woman said to me, 'You know something, Karina, I think this spiritual path has nothing to do with me. It's not for me.' So she gave up this spiritual journey.

"As I thought about what had happened, I realized that each person has his or her own nature and their relationship with the universe. I also realized that there are several religions and spiritual paths that meet the needs of each person according to his or her level of consciousness. Although we all walk the road of life, each one has his or her baggage, stories, and experiences. Ingrid already said that the Soul is an individual entity.

"I remember joining the Spiritual Freedom in December, and Ingrid left Brazil in April of the following year. I felt abandoned because I had no one else to talk to about this life of spiritual searching, this desire to discover the answer to the usual question, hidden in the recesses of the Soul, 'Who am I?' A few months later, sharing my experiences with two friends, they became interested and signed up. The three of us were longtime friends. I was thrilled to share this spiritual aspect of life with them.

"A funny thing happened right after I joined this path. I started talking about it to everyone I met, inviting them to participate as well. One day, while I was talking about it to a woman, I was surprised with a question. She asked me, 'Karina, tell me what these teachings really consist of.' I was a bit overwhelmed by not knowing how to put into words what I felt when I went to the inner temple. So I answered timidly, 'I don't know, I only know that it is good for me."

Karina had a short laugh and continued, "Months after this incident, I received a phone call from an Englishman who came to Rio to visit his uncle. He was half English and half Bolivian. It turns out that he was also a member of the Spiritual Freedom. The interesting thing is that he had planned to stay in Rio only for one month and ended up staying for three years. He was a wonderful help to me. We started giving talks together on the theme. It was a great partnership! As time went by, I got a lot of practice in talking about this path. And to finish the lectures, I always said, 'The Spiritual Freedom teaches us that the Soul is individual and that It exists because God loves It.' Can you see, Paulo, how the universe conspires in favor of each Soul? For thirty-two years, I sought the Spiritual Freedom and went through several experiences, which today I call 'connecting diamonds.' They are events of our life that have invisible lines, connecting them as part of a divine plan."

Paulo remained silent for a few seconds and finally said, "How interesting! Thank you so much for sharing this with me. Your story explains why you are so balanced and loving."

— I can only thank the universe for all these connecting diamonds. That's why I like to tell people that there is this possibility for spiritual growth.

Karina and Paulo walked a little further among the lush vegetation in the Botanical Garden. Looking at the trees, Karina could feel the pulse of life in the moving leaves. After some time, they said goodbye, promising to meet again soon.

The wound is the place where the light enters you.
Rumi

XIX
A treasure

In March 1980, on the first day of class, Paulo was waiting for a teacher along with his new classmates. He was a new student at that school. Renata was sitting on a chair near the entrance to the classroom. Paulo had looked at her before entering. It was at that moment that his interest in Renata began. She was reading a novel. She was so focused that she didn't realize that someone had noticed her.

The only chair available was on the other side of the classroom. Paulo sat down there. All the students were talking and making a lot of noise. They didn't even notice the newcomer. Paulo took a notebook and a pen from his backpack and suddenly heard, "What's up, newbie?" It was Helio. He and Paulo would become good friends later.

— Cool, and you? — Paulo answered with a serious tone.

— Everything is great, bro!

Helio said nothing more and joined the rest of the class. The teacher entered the classroom, and the class went on as usual. The teacher didn't realize that there was a newbie there either, and he didn't even ask. He did nothing more than teach the class, sitting in front of the students. He rarely looked at them, just reading the material from a book. He spent the whole class in this way, presenting the History of Brazil. Neither did the students pay any attention to the teacher. Apart from Paulo, the only students who paid attention to the teacher were Renata and Beatriz, her best friend.

From the other side of the classroom, Paulo realized how seriously Renata took her studies. He found this surprising, since the teacher himself did not seem to like what he was teaching.

At some point, the bell rang, announcing the break. The students rushed out of the room. The teacher was even faster than the students. It seemed that he had been forced to teach those youngsters. So he left like a rocket chasing the stars. On the other hand, the students regarded the break as a truce because attending classes was as if they were in a war. Therefore, the bell at the end of each class caused immense joy.

That day, the students crowded the school cafeteria. Not feeling hungry, Paulo thought he would wait for the delicious lunch prepared by Doce, his maid. In the courtyard, there was a bench under a mango tree. He sat there and began to watch the comings and goings of his classmates. Renata was on the classroom porch, and her hair was blowing in the gently moving breeze. From afar, she shone like the sun. At that moment, Paulo knew in his heart that he had just found a gem, which he should take care and preserve for the rest of his life.

As he sat there quietly, his gaze met Renata's and didn't turn away. He felt he had known her for a long time. Maybe it was a memory from past lives. But what mattered was that he realized that there were no secrets between them. So he let out a discreet sigh, which created the invisible bridge of love, the road that united his universe with Renata's. Then, love conquered the schoolyard, playing its melody in their hearts. Love was everywhere, and yet only Paulo and Renata realized it. With their eyes full of tenderness, the two looked at each other passionately, and thus the link between them was made without any words being said.

After a moment, Renata became embarrassed and left the balcony. With his heart quickly beating, almost coming out of his chest, Paulo turned his eyes to the clear sky and thanked for having met his Soul mate, the love of his life. At least, that's what he thought at that moment, unaware that the future always has a card up its sleeve.

The bell rang again, and the students hurried back to their classes. Paulo did not rush because he believed he knew what was necessary for him to live well. In his thoughts, he only needed Renata's love. He knew what had to be done to satisfy this sudden passion. As he walked from the courtyard to his classroom, he remembered a poet who declared, "Love, a mysterious, invisible treasure, always by our side, wanting to love us now and forever. For those who seek it on the path of life, they only need to look and listen with their heart." And, yes, Paulo had opened the eyes of his heart and looked upon the beautiful Renata, sparkling like a diamond. Finally, he arrived at the classroom. He had just sat down when Helio appeared. His colleague started speaking in a very direct way.

— I know you like Renata. I just want to tell you that she is a very staunch Catholic. I see her at Mass every Sunday. She never talks to boys and never dates anyone. Her mother guards her like the dog that won't let go of its bone. She just wants to study and be the best student in the class.

Helio did not realize that everything he had just said only made Paulo like Renata even more. Paulo liked fine, calm, and well-mannered girls. Renata was one of them, and besides, she never stopped smiling. Paulo just asked his classmate, "Is she the best student in the class?"

— Yes. It's always been her, since we were kids. I went to elementary school with her. She does nothing but study. I just wanted to warn you not to waste your time with her.

After listening to his colleague, Paulo smiled with satisfaction. The math teacher entered the room, and Helio had to return to his desk. Paulo felt that Renata looked like his mother Alice, a strong and independent woman. Despite her husband's inheritance, she pursued her dreams. There was only one thing she had longed for and had not succeeded in. She wanted to work in the health field. However, this did not come about because she had an operation on her eyes just before the university entrance exam date. This unexpected event separated her from her dream. However, she was not discouraged. She took a professional hairdressing course and became the most qualified person in the neighborhood. Men's or women's hair, straight or curly, she always had the secret for the best cut. Besides being a hairdresser, Alice also had an entrepreneurial side. Soon after starting her salon, she realized that women liked to take care of their bodies too. Where she lived, people valued the physical aspect very much, and Alice saw this as an opportunity to establish herself. Her ambition, although opportunistic, was not excessive. She just wanted to help women be themselves — beautiful, emancipated, and self-confident. So she rented the store next to the salon and started selling clothes, boots, and shoes of all kinds, watches, sunglasses, and jewelry. Alice's creativity went further still when she started selling cell phones and accessories. The salon and the store were known and loved by everyone in the neighborhood.

While the math teacher was speaking about equations, Paulo listed in his mind the achievements of his enterprising mother and tried to find similarities between her and Renata. Because Renata was the best in their class, Paulo saw in her the reflection of his mother. Therefore, he nourished even more in his heart his interest in her, which had just come into existence. When the teacher asked the students to form small groups, Paulo formed a group with Renata and Beatriz. This is how Renata and Paulo became friends. Years later, they started dating and ended up getting married.

XX
Queen of the home

It was Renata's birthday. Paulo and Beatriz were the only guests from their class. In addition to them, there were a few of Renata's cousins. Among them was Charlotte, Paulo's girlfriend. The guests went up to the terrace, where there was a space with food and drinks for the party. Renata's mother, seeing Paulo among the guests, said, "Here comes the king." And, indeed, Paulo felt like a king, but deep in his heart, he was missing his queen. Although he liked Charlotte's French way, his heart belonged to Renata. He and Renata had a strong feeling for each other. However, they could not show it. In front of everyone, they were just friends because her parents didn't want her to date so early.

Paulo had already told Renata many times that he liked her. She always replied, "I like you too." Despite all this shared interest, Paulo did not want to wait to have his first girlfriend. Furthermore, he did not want to be with a person he could not love freely. That's why when Charlotte wanted to date him, he did not hesitate. At a certain moment, he even thought he could forget Renata. Poor Paulo! Like everyone in love, he needed more time to realize that love has its own logic. A loving being once said, "Love is a feeling that comes to you when you don't plan, a feeling that you have when you don't understand." Others simply say that love is God. Anyway, young people don't think much about the meaning of love. They love, they fall in love, and most of the time, they confuse friendship with love. Paulo was like that too.

Renata did not mind Paulo's relationship with her cousin. After all, she and Paulo were just friends. Once, he asked her, "Doesn't my relationship with Charlotte bother you?"

— No! Why would that bother me? I'm happy for both of you.

Paulo was not only surprised, but also felt offended by Renata's reply. He thought she did not like him anymore. If she did, she would have felt uncomfortable with the situation. The truth is that Renata was wise in her actions. Inwardly, she liked Paulo, and that was enough for her. That's why she did not care about anything else. And why be affected by their relationship? Charlotte did not date anyone for very long. When she was in France, she would date a Frenchman. When she came to Rio to spend her vacation, she would date a boy from Rio. Her dates were like teenagers' adventures. One day, she would go to the movies with someone and the next, she wouldn't want to do it anymore. She dated so many boys that Renata lost count. Paulo was just one of those summer loves, who learned some French words from the beautiful and refined Charlotte. The latter was all French, all chic. Paulo learned to form a pout when pronouncing "tu" and "plus". Now he could say, "Je t'aime, cherie de mon Coeur" (I love you, my dear heart). It was the first thing he would say to Charlotte when they met. All happy and smiling, she answered, "Oh! Mon lapin doré, je t'aime bien aussi" (Oh! My golden rabbit, I like you too). Renata looked at them and said nothing. Every so often, she would laugh at Paulo. Since she was fluent in French, she knew what Paulo did not. She knew that "Je t'aime bien" means "to like" as a good friend and not "to love" as a boyfriend. So during two months of dating, Charlotte saw Paulo just as a friend, who was a lot of fun to kiss. Even though Renata knew about it, she kept quiet and didn't say anything to her friend Paulo. In fact, she never spoke neither of her thoughts nor of the things she wanted. She had learned to keep everything in her heart, as her mother had taught her. In childhood, she used to see her mother withdraw whenever her father spoke with an intimidating voice. It was in this family context, where the woman's voice is silenced, that Renata had learned to be a woman in society.

One evening, while Renata and Paulo were returning home from school, he told her that Charlotte had broken up with him a few days before going back to France.

— Really? — Renata pretended she didn't know.

— Yes, she did. But do you know what's interesting about all this?

— No!

— I got angry and said that I always liked you more than her.

— What did she say?

— She just smiled and answered, "OK!" I don't think she has ever felt anything for me all that time. She was just playing with me.

— But why are you complaining? You didn't really love her either. Isn't that right?

— At first, yes. However, with time, I began to like her.

— I see! — Renata paused for a moment. — And was she OK?

— Yes, she was. Actually, she was only thinking about her return to France.

— That's the way she is.

— Didn't you mind seeing me with her? I have asked you this several times, but now, tell me the truth — Paulo said with a serious look.

— You know very well that I can only date after joining the university. Paulo, listen! I like you a lot, but we must remain friends for now. Then we'll see what to do. The university is only a year away — Renata said cheerfully.

— True. It's only a short time away — said Paulo serenely.

Paulo always believed in Cupid, the messenger of love. He also believed in the theory of Soul mates and was convinced that Renata was his chosen one. On the other hand, he associated Renata's characteristics with his mother's creativity. He did not realize that what he liked about Renata was, in fact, what she had in common with his mother Alice.

The years passed. Paulo and Renata started dating, and some time, later they got married. After the wedding, circumstances arose that led Renata to give up her studies. In this way, she resigned herself to the role of queen of the home, coordinating the work of the maids. Coming from a traditional family, she could not see another possibility for her life. She never forgot what her mother had told her right after the wedding ceremony, "Learn how to take care of your husband in the best possible way. From today on, he is your world. Be a good housewife. In that way, Paulo will always be in love with you."

— I understand, Mom — Renata answered, happy to be married to a longtime friend.

People say it is always good to marry a person you really know. So, Renata thought, "Why not a longtime friend?" However, can we know a person entirely? In that case, is it possible to foresee things when you live in a world where nothing is permanent?

Renata behaved exactly as her mother had advised her. She became a person totally dedicated to her family. Unfortunately, things did not turn out as she expected. Although she did everything to make the marriage work, Paulo no longer loved her. Out of nowhere, they both began to see the marriage fall apart. They were unable to do anything against this.

Without even realizing it, the love that united them evaporated, and with it their marriage collapsed. Now there were nothing but ruins left from the promises made on the day they were united.

Meanwhile, they never gave up on themselves. They tried, in every way, to dress up a relationship that was already dead inside, but their efforts were not successful. They wanted to do this, mainly because of their children, but they could not change the situation.

XXI
A ship without passengers

In no way could Renata be different from her mother, who lived only to please her husband. She grew up in that kind of family where women are allowed to be themselves only in their minds. She had many dreams but did not have the courage to tell others about them. Perhaps her attitude was caused by her father's behavior, who usually spoke to the family members in an authoritarian tone.

Had it been up to her, and not to the thoughts of others, Renata would have gone to the faculty of engineering. She once commented on this with her father.

— What kind of engineer do you want to be? — her father asked.

— I don't know yet — Renata answered.

— How many women do you know who do this kind of work?

— There are many.

Her father was a successful lawyer and had already placed his eldest son as a partner in their family office. He then continued, "Since we have many lawyers in our family, why don't you become a lawyer?" Renata had not even considered this. When she was young, her father always said, "The science of law is for those who have courage." And when he talked about courage, he did not include women. "They are too delicate for that," he added. That's why Renata never thought about becoming a lawyer. At her core, she knew she could take all kinds of courses. She could even be a NASA employee if she wanted to. But eventually, she joined the faculty of arts, following her mother's steps. She was still at the beginning of the faculty when she became pregnant with Ana Paula. She had to leave the program in the middle of the year because she was having a difficult pregnancy. When Ana Paula was born, she did not go back to the university anymore. She chose to stay at home to be a good mother, and so she was a mother for many years, even when Ana Paula and her younger brother Rafael had become adults and didn't need her anymore. Her only duty then was to supervise the maids. Over the years, Renata grew into this role, and now she could not escape it anymore.

Unfortunately, Paulo wanted his wife to be more than that. He wanted Renata to have a steady job like his mother had. He had fallen in love with a different Renata, a strong and intelligent Renata. Now she did not lead the life that she seemed to be destined for. She had become an uninteresting woman. When she wasn't taking care of the housework, she would sit on the sofa, watching several TV shows. When Paulo came home at night, he did not like to see his wife like that. As time went by, he distanced himself from this new version of Renata. She was no longer the best at the things she did. The more Paulo kept this feeling of disappointment inside himself, the more his love for her diminished. Besides not loving her as before, he nurtured a certain resentment in his heart, as if she had deceived him. It must be because he was not aware that people change over time. There came a point in their marriage when he no longer wanted to go out with her or even talk to her. When he returned from work, he had dinner and went to sleep. In addition to avoiding her, he got angry about anything she said or did, even when she tried to be funny. He really changed his behavior toward her. When the situation reached the point where Renata could not stand it anymore, they started treating each other like strangers, living in the same apartment. So the years went by, and the passion between them dissipated.

Some people think that love comes ready-made, like a magic trick. In such cases, passion usually ends from one moment to another, as suddenly as it began. Other people perceive love as something that is built over time, a little plant that needs to be constantly watered. During twenty-eight years of marriage, Paulo and Renata's love just withered away until it no longer existed.

Many years after getting married, Renata realized that marriage does not make a woman a fulfilled person. Sometimes she would sit on Ipanema Beach and reflect on all this. In her thoughts, she blamed her mother, who had made her believe that every woman had to get married to deserve a place in society.

At home, the atmosphere was getting heavier. Paulo saw his wife as a failure, but he never expressed words of disappointment. For many years, he pretended to be happy with his marriage and disguised his discontent until he could no longer do so. Finally, he accepted that he was not happy and began to complain about his wife in his thoughts. On the other hand, Renata would also like to be somewhere sophisticated, being part of an important project. Instead, there she was in that fancy apartment in Ipanema, taking care of the house, without any prospect of fulfilling herself. As the years went by, she saw her personality fade away little by little. She became her husband's shadow. No longer able to put up with this feeling of self-deception, she gave in to the sadness of a frustrated marriage. Over the years, their marriage sank like a ship without passengers, lost in the middle of the ocean.

Even though Renata couldn't stand this monotonous life, she did not have the courage to talk to Paulo about it. Thus, the two remained married and unhappy for years, dealing in silence with their respective frustrations. After Paulo was fired, he spent a few days at home and things got worse. The resentment turned into words that hurt. Without either of them realizing it, arguments started to replace conversations.

One day, while they were fighting, Renata said to Paulo, "You stole twenty-eight years of my life. I could be doing some decent work. Instead, I stayed in this apartment, cut off from my dreams."

Paulo was taken aback. In fact, he had not asked Renata to stay home. If she accepted her role as a housewife, it was because she believed that her life had to be like that. Paulo, however, always wanted his wife to be an independent and fulfilled woman. He then replied, "I never asked you to stay home. I also thought you didn't do the right thing by following your mother's advice and going to the Faculty of Arts."

— Why didn't you say anything?

— I thought you wanted to follow in your mother's footsteps.

— You could have said what you thought. You never say what you think. I can't take it anymore.

— It was no use saying anything. You wouldn't have understood.

— You know very well that I couldn't go to class anymore with that difficult pregnancy. You, on the other hand, continued with your School of Economics as if everything were normal.

After twenty-eight years of marriage, it was only on that day that they honestly shared their frustrations. Unfortunately, this honesty, which had been waiting for so long to be exposed, came with the sorrows that had accumulated over the years. Sometimes it was a lack of kindness, other times a misplaced word or a heavy but deafening silence.

At any rate, Renata couldn't stand the wounds of the past anymore. All this time, she had kept the sadness in her core. Now, she didn't want to hide her disappointment anymore to honor their marriage promises. She then exploded in tears. With her eyes wet, she turned away from Paulo, hiding her face with her hands.

Paulo said in a calm voice, "You never told me you wanted to continue your studies."

— It's because you never asked. And how could I have done that? You used to come home from the university all happy that I was pregnant. So I preferred to keep things to myself.

Paulo felt sorry for her and did not know what to do. He simply said, "So what are we going to do now?"

Renata looked at him and answered, "What we should have done a long time ago."

When you give up your freedom to maintain a marriage, the union itself becomes a kind of emotional prison. Thus, Renata had felt imprisoned for many years. She had been deprived of her dreams and aspirations since she got pregnant for the first time.

Paulo approached her and said, "So let's separate. I'll find a place to live, and you can keep the apartment. And I want you to know that I've always wanted the best for you."

Without saying a word, Renata agreed. She knew that Paulo was a balanced man, and that the sudden decision to separate was the right thing to do at that stage of their lives. What had worked between them had already played out. Now, they needed to move on. They embraced and said goodbye. It was a fraternal hug because, after all, they had been friends since before they were married. Soon after, Paulo left their apartment.

XXII
Mother's Day

Karina and Paulo were sitting near the beach, on the same bench as always. In front of them, the sea stretched out without limits. The wind churned its surface, and its movement called to mind the impermanence of life as its waves rose in fury, then gently subsided. The sun's rays, mirrored in the infinite blue of the ocean, turned the landscape golden.

Paulo started the conversation, "I am concerned about my children's future. But the truth is that I don't know what to tell them at this moment when my personal life is not well-defined. I used to say that to succeed in life, they had to follow in my footsteps."

— You don't have to do well in life to advise your children — answered Karina.

— I agree, but I find it difficult to face them and show them which directions to take.

— Why do you think so?

— Because we are not very close. When I separated from Renata, they took her side. That's normal because I was never present in their lives. It's funny how we replicate what we criticize in others. My parents never supported my childhood dreams. And today I see myself acting the same way with my children, mainly with Rafael.

— Try to talk to them, not as a father, but as a friend. Listen without making judgments. Tell them that you are not always right, and that they can always count on you. Tell them that you love them, regardless of what they do or don't do. Share with them that what really matters is knowing that they are happy.

— I am deeply grateful for these tips.

— I should thank you for being my friend.

Paulo thought for a while and finally said, "I wonder if there is a way to deal with the fear parents have for their children."

— I didn't have any kids in this life, but I think the fear of parents for their children can't be too different from other fears. Generally, when I feel fear, I reassure myself by listening to the voice of the Inner Master. He makes me see a solution.

— Like a creative idea when facing a threat?

— Exactly!

— Can you give me an example of such an experience?

— Yes — said Karina excitedly.

She then started sharing one of her stories. Paulo listened attentively.

— One day, after having lunch with my mother on Mother's Day, we went for a drive. The problem was that I forgot to roll up the windows when we stopped at a traffic light. It's important to do that because there are numerous muggings at traffic lights. Suddenly, out of nowhere, a street kid appeared and said, "Auntie, pass your wallet, or I'll blow up your car." My mother got scared and started screaming for help. But nobody lifted a finger. Then I had a creative idea and told the boy, "Not today! Today is Mother's Day." He smiled and answered, "You're right, auntie. Bye!" Not realizing that the boy had already left, my mother kept shouting for help. I had to tell her that the situation had already been resolved. That's how we avoided being mugged that day.

— Unbelievable!

— Unbelievable and very funny!

They had a great laugh, and then Paulo went on, "Very funny now, but I can imagine it wasn't like that at the moment."

— That's right, especially for my mother.

— I can see how important it is to learn to be calm at any moment of our lives — said Paulo.

— We must always be tuned to our inner self and realize that there is always a way out.

— True!

Karina had to leave. They said goodbye, and Paulo went back home. As he walked, he felt his heart rejoice in this new friendship. He was happy and constantly smiling. In his heart, he thanked every step he took on his way back home, back to God.

Do everything you have to do, but not with greed, not with ego, not with lust, not with envy but with love, compassion, humility, and devotion.

Shree Krishna

XXIII
The poem of the universe

Paulo had disobeyed his parents in becoming an economist. Rafael, his son, acted against his will in becoming a poet. Paulo did not want to accept this reality, but deep down he knew that his son's Soul had always been that of a poet.

Some years earlier, when Rafael was a teenager, Paulo used to take him for walks through the streets of Rio. During these strolls, when the two of them came across colossal highways or building constructions, he would say to his son, "Do you see this building? It was made by architects and engineers. You know, my son, only a few artists make enough money to support themselves." Rafael just looked and agreed, without realizing why his father said that. Paulo tried to influence his son to follow a career with guaranteed success. He wanted his son to be an engineer, and he paid for a course at one of the best faculties of engineering in the United States. Paulo wasted a lot of money trying to realize his dream through his son. However, the reality was different. Rafael went on to study telecommunications engineering in Boston and was even one of the best students in his class. Everything went well when he suddenly dropped out in his last year and returned to Rio. He wanted to pursue a career as a writer and poet.

Paulo was devastated by his son's decision. He did not hesitate to say that the latter acted foolishly. One day, they had a severe confrontation, and Rafael left home.

— Do you really think you can live off your art in a society like ours?

Rafael, who lived his art in everything he did, could not say anything without a little poetry. He answered, "Dad, although many don't have eyes to see the beauty of the universe or ears to hear its beautiful song, its poem keeps sounding. I see things that way."

— I wonder how you will survive without my support. I won't be here to take care of you forever. Now that you are an adult, either you conform to my will, or you will make your life somewhere else.

Thereafter, Paulo went to work and when he returned, he didn't see his son anymore. As his daughter Ana Paula had already left home when she got married, Paulo and Renata lived alone in that huge apartment.

Renata supported Rafael, and he left home searching for his dreams. At the time, he was dating a girl he would later marry. Her name was Bianca. Before meeting Rafael, she had searched in vain for a man who saw life as a poem. She and Rafael met in a bar near N. S. da Paz Square. There, they talked all night. The next day, they continued talking. The months passed, and at the end of the year, they discovered that the tree of love had grown without their noticing. Between the two of them, nothing went fast, it was all simple, all natural. At the beginning of the following year, they were united both in spirit and heart.

Rafael saw life in the universe as a great poem, and Bianca loved him for being like that. She felt that few men could be compared to him. He lived fully in the present moment with great expectations for the future.

Bianca was an independent and financially accomplished girl. She was also very intelligent because at only twenty-two years old, she had passed a public examination to become an expert in environmental crime. When Rafael left home, she didn't hesitate to invite him to live with her.

Despite having her feet on the ground, Bianca was also a born poet. However, she needed more experience to realize the poetry within herself. That's why she loved to sit next to Rafael on the balcony on starry nights, listening to him reciting poems. They sprang from his heart, flowing from him with love and passion. They were part of the infinite poem of the universe. She looked at him softly and fell more and more in love with him. She got lost in his poetry, and Raphael in her gaze.

They loved each other sincerely and, thanks to the poem of the universe, they enlivened the fire of passion that united them. This often happened on that balcony of Bianca's apartment. Rafael knew many poems by heart and gestured like a king in his palace. He and his sublime declamations formed a unity.

It was always like this between the two of them until Bianca got pregnant. After the baby was born, nothing changed. Rafael himself had already said, "Love is the stream that permeates everything in life." Rafael lived in a dream, and Bianca, even though she was more connected to reality, dreamed with him. At her core, she believed that one day, the world would remember her favorite poet.

Going back to the time when Rafael lived in Boston, before starting thinking about the poem of the universe, he was very dedicated to his studies. He liked his engineering course very much, always getting high marks. He didn't drink or smoke, but he would go out with his friends on the weekends because he enjoyed their company.

In his field of study, there was a lot of calculus, and he was always passionate about mathematics. He also liked music. One day, Marc, one of his American friends, invited him to enroll in some piano lessons.

— Rafael, I want to learn to play the piano. Would you like to come along?

Rafael was interested because once he had heard someone say that music is the mathematics of waves. He enrolled in pure curiosity. Until that moment, the idea of living from art had never crossed his mind.

On the first day of class, Abdul, a professor from India, played Beethoven's *Moonlight Sonata* and talked about many things, except the piano. At one point, he said that a good musician had to know the poem of the universe, and that music and poetry express themselves with the same language. He also pointed out that the verses of this universal poem were infinite. Finally, he added that parts of these verses were found in some books, such as those that tell the stories of ancient civilizations.

Rafael was amazed at what his professor had said. Taken by a strange enthusiasm, he went to him at the end of the class and asked, "Can you recommend one of the books that contain verses from the poem of the universe? I mean the books about ancient civilizations"

— Sure! — said the professor, his face illuminated.

Abdul took a book out of his backpack, handed it to Rafael and said, "This is a gift. I hope you like it!" Rafael was so happy that he didn't realize the book was already old and received the gift with an open heart. They smiled at each other, and it was right at that moment that Rafael's destiny entirely changed course. Although he didn't know it, he was not the same anymore. However, he still needed a few months to discover himself.

That very day, he began reading the book he had been given. The title was *Ramayana*, a Hindu epic poem recounted by William Buck. *Ramayana*, which means The Way of Rama, tells an ancient story, over two thousand years, in which Prince Rama, a hero, overcomes evil by using Love.

Although he really liked the achievements of the enlightened Rama, Rafael did not have a good reading discipline. He would usually read sporadically. Sometimes he would go for more than three weeks without reading even a page. So, months went by, until the day a quote from the book aroused his interest. In the chapter *"The Invisible Warrior"[1]*, the first paragraph said:

Don't regret the way the sky spins up there,
For the sky will last long enough without you.
I am all that,
All this Life;
I am all of this.

Rafael stopped for a moment and asked himself, "Who is behind all this? Who is all this Life? Who created heaven and time? As for me, why do I exist?" Thus, he embarked upon the great questions of life. He closed his eyes and realized that he was no longer the same. He felt like a man apart from the world, a leaf that was detached from the tree of humanity, or even a branch that no longer swung to the beautiful pleasure of the wind. When he opened his eyes, he saw that there was no one around to answer these questions. He then decided to follow his own path, constantly searching for the best verses of the poem of the universe — verses of the spirit that might give him answers.

Two months after that experience, he left the engineering course and returned to Rio. While Renata was supporting her son's decision, Paulo suffered a lot from this situation. He was devastated, and the atmosphere at home got worse every day. Finally, Rafael felt bad about his father's condition and enrolled in Law School. He graduated after a few years but did not want to take the Bar Exam at the Lawyers Organization of Brazil. Once again, Paulo suffered because of this. He did everything to show his son that living from

---

[1] Ramayana, BUCK, William. São Paulo: Ed. CULTRIX, 1995, p. 337.

art was not a good option. His suggestions did not help because his son had decided to be a poet, and nothing could deter him.

In fact, Rafael had done nothing but respond to the call of his Soul. Now he lived with Bianca, his wife and admirer. They had a daughter, and with her, they lived in the present moment, dreaming of better days in the future.

XXIV
Dreaming

Lately, Rafael felt he was receiving a lot of love and support from the universe, and thus had faith in what he was doing. He knew that the day would come when the things he wrote would be engraved in the hearts of many people, whom he might never meet.

Today he received a message from Ana Paula, his sister. Among his family members, she was the only person who behaved in a strange way — she would disappear and appear suddenly when people needed her most. She had developed this habit to protect herself from her parents. It turns out that Renata and Paulo thought that Ana Paula's personal affairs were theirs too. Like all parents, they cared a lot about their children's welfare. The only problem was that sometimes they were not aware they invaded her space. When Ana Paula realized that, she shut herself off and did not talk about her issues anymore. From then on, no one else in the family knew what was going on with her and her husband. When the family got together, she smiled and never talked about herself. Initially, Renata and Paulo found her behavior weird and were very concerned about her. As the years went by, Ana Paula kept smiling at the family gatherings, convincing her parents of her happiness. Finally, they accepted their daughter's discretion and learned to respect her space.

At that moment in Rafael's life, he really needed to hear something positive from his sister. So Ana Paula, who always showed up when she was needed, sent him a message.

On WhatsApp, she said:

[Good morning, my beloved brother. I hope you're doing well. Look, you cannot stop writing the verses of the universal poem. You cannot stop dreaming because the world belongs to those who keep dreaming. I love you.]

Rafael had just woken up. When he saw his sister's message, he was perplexed and happy at the same time — a feeling hard to explain. Then he called her, and they talked for over an hour. At the end of the call, he asked, "What made you send me this motivational message today?"

— I had a dream, and in it there were many people who were buying a book called *The Poem of the Universe*. When I woke up, I reflected a lot on it, and I realized that the author of that book could only be you.

At that moment, many thoughts went through Rafael's mind. However, he didn't know which was the right one to express what he was feeling. Thrilled, he just exclaimed, "How interesting!"

— That's right! I must go now.

— OK! Take care!

— You too!

Soon after talking to his sister, Rafael sat on his bed and thought about the conversation he had had with her. His thoughts became serene, and he imagined the whole world manifesting itself.

This world was like a sleeping sea. Rafael looked at the beauty of the waters and realized that the waves ceased to exist at that moment. The sea was static, totally calm. In this short space of time like a breath, everything seemed immobile, immutable, permanent, and as eternal as Love.

When Raphael returned from this reverie, his heart jumped with joy. He then turned on the computer and started writing a play called *Beyond the Horizon*.

XXV
Love

A few months after writing the play *The horizon*, Rafael received a call from his father. They had spoken only occasionally over the previous years. During all that time, Rafael's understanding of life had matured a great deal. He had changed a lot as a person but did not change anything in his convictions. He read and wrote at every free moment. He was one of those who never give up on life, those whose dreams resist cold and heat. Deep in his heart, he knew that one day the future would prove him right.

Paulo had also matured. Since he had met his good friend Karina, his life was no longer the same. Without realizing it, the burden of past hurts no longer weighed so heavily on him. Little by little, he was changing spiritually and becoming a better version of himself.

When Paulo called his son, he said, "Hi, Rafael! How are you?"

— I'm fine, Dad. And you? We haven't spoken for a long time!

— I'm fine too. What about meeting today in the late afternoon?

— I'd love to!

— Great!

— What about in Copacabana on the sidewalk near the beach around five o'clock?

— Yes, we can meet outside the Copacabana Palace Hotel.

— It's a deal!

They met near the beach at the agreed time. The sea was there as always, immutable and infinite. At that time of day, it seemed to rest while the waves moved calmly. In this dance, which was drawn on the surface, the waters came and went tirelessly, kissing the warm sand.

Paulo invited his son to have a guarana at one of the kiosks by the sea. An unexpected and soft breeze began to blow, bringing a feeling of well-being and love. Paulo started the conversation.

— How are things going with you?

— I'm doing well. I'm also thrilled to be here with you now. I'm glad to know that you are no longer resentful of me.

— All I ever wanted was your happiness, a difficult thing to find nowadays.

— I know, Dad. I even spoke with Bianca a few days ago about our disagreement. She made me see things differently.

— How is she doing?

— She's fine.

— Is she still supporting you?

— Yes, and I'm sure the day will come when all this sacrifice will have been worth it.

— And how are you organizing your professional life?

— Lately I have been staying at home during the day taking care of our daughter. At night, I try to do something about my art, always writing my poems, novels, and plays.

— Do you still want to follow your career as a poet and writer?

— Yes, I do, Dad. Unfortunately, I am not like most men.

— I can't understand you.

— Don't worry about me. I was born with the Soul of a poet, and there is nothing I can do about it. Who knows, one day I might live from my arts.

— What makes you think so?

— I make my art with my heart, not thinking about the rewards. This is because speaking or writing about Love is already the greatest reward. The rest is just a matter of time.

— So you don't consider the possibility of applying for a job in the government? Sergio, my former boss, told me that his son is now a prosecutor and lives very well.

— But what is it to live well, Dad?

Paulo did not know what to say, and Rafael continued.

— For a long time, I lied to myself about my professional career. Now I can't escape my nature anymore.

— It's something I don't understand much. I think I need to hear more about it.

— Dad, do you remember when I was in law school?

— Yes, I do.

— Once, while I was an intern in a public institution, I overheard a conversation between two of my bosses, agonizing over the years remaining before their retirement. At some point, one of them called Douglas looked at me and said, "Rafael, think carefully about what moves you when you choose the area in which you will work. Look at me! I've worked here for over twenty years. Look at this chair! I sit on it every day, and I've been doing the same things since I first entered this building. Do you believe that? It's no joke, I'm serious. I don't know how I don't go crazy with all this, sitting in the same corner all these years. I can't take it anymore." A few days after this incident, another intern told me that my boss had a good salary. So she thought he was complaining for no reason. I still remember the first day of my internship. Douglas tried to please me by showing the photos of his international trips with his family. Everything was wonderful in the photos, and they looked delighted. In the days that followed, at work, he made it a habit to always share with me the adventures from these trips. The more he talked about them, the happier he was. And when he didn't talk about these things, he seemed sad. Instead of dedicating himself to what he really liked to do, Douglas preferred to remain in his comfort zone. Somehow, this gave him the assurance of a better life. However, he was not a happy public servant, and all of us in the office knew it. He kept complaining about life, wishing for his retirement as soon as possible. He never felt fulfilled in that job.

At that moment, Paulo felt sorry for Douglas. He already had a similar experience when he worked as an economist. So, he knew how painful it was to devote oneself to something that did not please one's heart. In his case, economics never really fulfilled him. At the time he worked, he used to compare his frustration to the joy he felt, when he was painting the beauties of the world as a child. That, indeed, filled his heart with joy.

Rafael asked, "So Dad, again — What is to live well? Working just to survive?"

Paulo just listened.

Serene, Rafael continued.

— Even if art today is not as valuable as it used to be, I don't want to start a journey other than my own by doing something that doesn't fulfill me. Otherwise, my passage on earth would be a lie — he took a brief pause and said — The truth is that I can't fit into an environment where people relate to each other according to their appearance. By working with art, I feel more connected to myself.

— Son, that's the way the world is. We usually don't follow our hearts. But if you don't have a steady job, how will you support your family?

— I don't worry much about this because I know there are still many stories to experience. Every day, I contemplate life outside and inside me and write down the things I perceive, the truths of the Soul. On the other hand, I am aware that the literary market has become superficial because many write only what sells the most. I refuse to do that. Anyway, there will be a moment when my sun will shine. God is in control! I feel it in my heart.

— Son, you don't go to church, nor do you have a fixed religion, but you always talk about God.

— God is everything, Dad. God is Love.

— What do you mean?

— It's because after searching a lot without finding God anywhere, I concluded that It is Love, nothing more, nothing less. Love has no price, it is the only thing that is given and received with joy, the only thing that is free in this world. To have it in our lives, we just need to be true to ourselves.

— Hearing you talking about love reminds me of Plato's *Symposium*, a wonderful treatise on this subject.

— By the way, Love is much more than anything our mind is capable of conceptualizing. That's why I like to think that God is Love.

— I believe I have much to learn from you, my son. Now I am more positive about your future. I don't think there can be a better life than the one you live by writing and talking about Love. You know, I'm pleased to hear you today.

— Thanks, Dad. Before I forget, I will be presenting one of my plays in two months. Would you like to come?

— That's great! I'd love to.

— Awesome! I brought two tickets for you — said Rafael, handing the tickets to his father.

— You know I don't have a girlfriend, right?

— I know, but I believe the right person can show up at any time or has already shown up.

They had a laugh. Paulo accepted the tickets and said, "Now go, my son! You know that the city is not safe at night."

— That's right! — Rafael agreed.

As he stood up, he looked at his father thoughtfully and added, "I'm happy to talk to you about my feelings. I always thought you wouldn't understand. But today, I find it very intriguing to see how the future can surprise us."

— Things change, my son.

— They really do! After all, life is like that, it's made of changes — Rafael said and left.

The sky was already getting dark. Rafael was happy to talk to his father again about his love for art, without any embarrassment. After some time, Paulo returned home. The next day, he was going to meet Karina. The conversations with her had become precious to him. For nothing in this world, would he miss the opportunity to be with his new friend to talk more about life.

XXVI
How Lucky!

Paulo and Karina agreed to meet at General Tiburcio Square, at Red Beach, a quiet place surrounded by hills and trees. Paulo waited for Karina near the square monument. With a meditative look, he contemplated the world around him.

That day was special because it gave Paulo a sense of stillness. Not far from him, was a couple exchanging caresses and talking about love. Paulo looked at them and asked himself, "Can death separate what love unites?" Instantly, thoughts began to stir in his mind. However, he did not let himself be conquered by them. He had already realized that in the turmoil of the spirit, no favorable answer is revealed. With a certain discernment, he came back to contemplate the beauty of nature around him.

The Babylon Hill stood behind the Sugar Loaf cable car station. This time, Paulo did not resist the temptation to think because the hill reminded him of Babylon in Mesopotamia. "Oh Babylon!" he murmured. It was a great city that had risen from the earth to dominate the world. Years later, it had been devoured by the same earth. Babylon makes us think of a wonderful and mighty city, like Athens, Giza, Rome, and many others. Like these cities, on one day, things are born; on another, they die. The same happens with people. That's life. "Everything that lives, dies, one day or another," Paulo thought. Then his thoughts faded, and his mind became quiet again. After a few minutes, Karina appeared. They began to walk.

Still at Red Beach, they could see the cable car taking many tourists to the Sugar Loaf Mountain. From up there, you can see the Guanabara Bay, Copacabana Beach, and Christ the Redeemer. As they had already gone up to the Sugar Loaf Mountain many times, they decided to walk to the Urca Seawall and enjoy the sunset with the view of the Guanabara Bay.

On their way, they talked about life. As they passed the Urca pier, Karina and Paulo noticed a compass rose, a mosaic composed of white, black, and brown Portuguese stones. Paulo was amazed by this work of art. Long before he met Karina, he did not feel the presence of God in the beautiful things of the world. Now he and his way of seeing things had changed.

Near the Urca pier, there were some people fishing and having a good time. They were happy, and Paulo was thankful to see this moment of pure joy. Moments like this are small details of everyday life that can change a feeling of sadness to that of contentment and happiness.

After a long walk, they decided to sit in a bar called The Girl from Urca and wait for the sunset.

Paulo spoke.

— Do you remember when I told you about my cousin Diego last time?

— Of course, I do.

— I told you that he was the light of our family. Today, speaking with you lights up my life. Many things have changed inside and outside me since I met you. Thank you for that.

— You're welcome — Karina thought for a while. — But you know, we are all conductors of light.

Paulo listened with a perplexed look. He did not disagree or agree with what Karina had said. He just wanted to understand this question of light a little more.

Karina continued.

— My father was an engineer for many years. It was a good job, but we couldn't afford anything extra. When I was born, he was invited to be an engineer for Banc of Brazil. This changed our lives. Years later, my mother told me it was at this time that we were able to buy our first washing machine. She thought that my coming into the world had brought a blessing to the family and said to me happily, "Karina, you are the light of our family." I believe that each one of us, to varying degrees, comes into this world with a light. All of us are part of a universal purpose, and to become aware of this purpose is to write a stanza of the poem of life.

— I remember that soon after I was born, my father received the funding to build his church. He used to say that I brought the light related to God's affairs in our lives. That must be why he was convinced that I should follow his church too.

— He must see this as an act of gratitude to God.

— Everything is clearer to me now.

— Great! You know, your family is very similar to mine.

— Were they also very religious?

— Yes, however, that was not a problem. When I became an adult and wanted to follow another path, they understood it perfectly. They respected my way of seeking God. We had a very harmonious relationship until they passed away. My father died sixteen years before my mother. He had a heart attack, and he was gone in a few minutes.

— Would you like to tell me the details?

— Sure! The three of us lived together in our apartment — my father, my mother and me because all my brothers had already gotten married and left home. I remember that one day, after taking a nap, my parents decided to go for a walk along the beach. Five minutes later, they came back, and my mother said, "Your father is not feeling well. I'm going to get him some coffee." My dad rested his head on my lap, and my mom brought a cup of coffee and called an ambulance. This happened on a Friday afternoon, and the traffic was terrible. The ambulance took a long time to get to our place. When it finally did, he had already passed away. I believe this was a good way of leaving life.

— Why do you think so?

— Because he dreaded the idea of being sick and bedridden for years. He was gone quickly and did not suffer. This situation was not good for us, but we managed to deal with his death in a harmonious way over time.

— And your mother? How did she die?

— She had an umbilical hernia because she had had six children. Her doctor once told her that there were two options regarding this hernia. She could undergo surgery, which was not very safe because of her age, or she could just live with it.

— What did she choose?

— She decided not to have the surgery. That year was hard for her because one of my brothers passed away. She was sad about his death, and consequently, the hernia became strangulated. She got into a coma for a fortnight before passing away.

— I'm sorry!

— Life is like that, made of moments of suffering and joy. We must always look at the good side of things. And the truth is that my mother lived in love with life. She was always happy, and her spirit was at peace.

Karina spoke about the sad events of her life with unparalleled serenity. Paulo watched her and could not understand how it was possible to talk so calmly about such painful things. He then thought, "Karina must not be an ordinary person." He was right because she was unique.

Anyway, Karina was different, and everything about her was pleasant. She talked about death with a light heart. Although this subject was a burden to Paulo's ears, she made it light. The smile that never left her face comforted all Souls around her. Paulo listened quietly and with curiosity.

Through Karina's attitude, he came to realize that there was no need to struggle against the sad events of life. Existence itself is made up of good and bad things, and there is nothing that can be done to prevent this duality. Life goes on, always loyal to its course, like a flowing river, sometimes agitated, sometimes gentle.

While listening to Karina, Paulo sensed that the most important thing is the way one reacts to day-to-day events, whether positive or negative.

Karina continued.

— My mother's life had always been quiet. Before she went to the afterlife, she lived with my sister in Brasília and led a normal life.

— It appears that she lived only to love life and take care of her children.

— That's right.

— Looking at it this way, I understand that there is always a good side to life's tragedies — Paulo concluded.

— Death should not be something that frightens us or brings us suffering. In some parts of the world, like Africa and Asia, people celebrate when a family member dies. We must learn to accept death as we accept life — Karina said.

— I fully agree. Now, back to the fact that your mother died while in a coma, I think she left the world in a gentle way too. I say that because I heard people compare a coma to a state of revelation.

— I think you're right — Karina said, reflective. — Anyway, she was at peace when she died. When I learned she had passed away without much suffering, I thought, "How lucky!"

Karina had to leave. She got up, and Paulo was quick to ask, "What are you doing tomorrow afternoon?"

— Nothing important. I may go for a walk — answered Karina immediately.

— I intend to visit my friend Vanessa at Café Sorriso. I can send you the address by WhatsApp if you want to come along. It would be very nice to introduce you to her. You will enjoy meeting her, and I think she will love talking to you too.

— That's a good idea. See you tomorrow then!

— Perfect!

Karina left. Paulo, as usual, was thoughtful for a few minutes before standing up. On the way home, he realized that everything in the universe is connected. Thus, he saw a certain synchronicity between his thoughts about Babylon and Karina's story. Both dealt with death, treating it as a natural process.

But deep down, Paulo was not very convinced of this thought yet. At some point, for some unknown reason, he felt the need to stop walking. Then he closed his eyes and, for a moment, had the feeling that the hand of God was behind all the events of life, somehow making it possible for everything to converge on one point — the origin of all existence.

XXVII
A school

After separating from Paulo, Renata was very sad, not because of the separation, but because she would have to start all over again. She did not have the confidence in herself to do it. Right after their separation, she stayed home and read. Sometimes she watched romantic movies, and when she finished, she cried because she was alone.

One day, she received a phone call from Eliane, a cousin she had not seen for a long time. Meeting her again brought a change in her routine. Eliane was very communicative, always happy, and never let anyone get sad around her. In addition, being thirty-five years old and single, she considered herself to be a woman in complete control of her life.

By being with her cousin, Renata slowly began to have more self-esteem. She then went back to taking care of herself, going to the university, and playing sports. On weekends, she was happy to be able to spend time out with someone as lively as her cousin. They had fun, doing a bit of everything, but mostly going to bars. Eliane encouraged her cousin, saying, "You must have more fun. Paulo must be having fun too." It was good that Eliane helped Renata to forget about Paulo.

One night, at a bar in town, while Renata sat quietly, pensive as always, Eliane exchanged a few kisses with her friend Luan. For months now, every time the two of them went out, Luan would appear out of nowhere to be with Eliane. One such evening, Renata asked her cousin about this relationship.

— Won't you get hurt with Luan?

— I know what I'm doing. I don't fall in love easily, and Luan is just a friend. He knows it's nothing serious.

— But are you sure you won't fall in love?

— Yes, I'm sure. I've already told you that we are friends. I'm a free spirit and I don't want to get attached to anyone right now.

— OK! I get it.

Eliane thought it was very natural to occasionally enjoy life with her friend Luan. One night, while the two cousins were at a restaurant, Eliane went to the restroom and took a long time to come back. Renata got worried and went looking for her. To her surprise, she discovered that her cousin was crying because of Luan. In fact, she had been crying over him for quite some time. It turned out that he had started dating another woman and stopped seeing her. Eliane missed him and soon realized that she really loved him. One day, when she logged on to Facebook, she saw Luan's dating status. She immediately sent him a message, questioning this sudden relationship, and he replied, "[First, we are just friends, and you didn't want anything serious. You said you are a free spirit, and you don't get attached to anyone. I met a woman who really likes me, and I'm happy with her. Please don't write to me anymore.]"

Renata had started going to bars with her cousin, trying to be an empowered woman. Now she was taking care of her mentor, who was crying over a man. In doing so, she realized that to be an empowered woman, she didn't have to go out bar-hopping every night. Besides, they had been doing this for eight months, and she never met a man who really interested her.

After crying for many days, Eliane decided to spend some time with an aunt in Florianopolis, saying that she needed a change of scenery to regain control of her life.

Renata stayed home again on weekends, and during the week, she went to the university. She read a lot, and in one of her books, an author compared life to a school — she said that life is a gift from God, offering many opportunities for growth.

From that moment on, Renata got into the habit of always thanking God for being alive. As time went by, she began to wake up feeling happy, whether it was because of a happy dream or a feeling of peace that had no explanation. She now began to see life as a precious jewel, which gave her great satisfaction.

XXVIII
In every corner

One morning, Renata called her cousin Charlotte, who lived in France. The two of them talked a lot and agreed that she would go to France to spend some time there. A few months later, Renata packed her bags and set out on this adventure.

— I'm so happy to see you! — Charlotte said excitedly, hugging her cousin when she met her at the airport.

— Me too!

A few days later, Charlotte asked Renata, "Do you remember Jean?"

— Yes, I do.

— We can visit him tomorrow. What do you think?

— That's a good idea.

Charlotte asked Renata not to mention anything about Jean's parents. "Cancer took both of them," she said with a sad look. After losing his parents, Jean became depressed and eventually separated from his wife. He also quit his job. And Charlotte, as a good neighbor, liked to organize little parties so as not to let her childhood friend remain in sadness.

Renata had known Jean for a long time. When she was nine years old, her parents wanted her to know a little of France. She spent two years there, studying in the same school as her cousin. In the first year of school, she sat next to Jean, and the two became good friends.

The night they visited Jean, Charlotte invited her boyfriend Homer to come along. He was from Benin, a country on the West Coast of Africa. Before dating Homer, Charlotte had had many boyfriends, but she had been now with this Beninese man for six years. When Renata asked her about her boyfriend, she answered, "Homer is the right person for me. Every day I learn to love him more and more, and he does the same."

In Jean's living room, they were all sitting around, talking. Renata could read the sadness and loneliness on Jean's face. Even though he was suffering, he smiled at his guests. In fact, he was always like that, smiling constantly.

That evening, Renata was the first to start the conversation, asking Homer some questions in French.

— Do people speak French in your country?

— Yes, but besides French, there are several other languages.

— How interesting! Benin must be a fascinating country, right?

— Yes, it is. Charlotte and I agreed to visit it at the end of this year.

— Is there room for one more? — Renata asked, pleased.

— Why not? It would be a wonderful adventure.

In the middle of the conversation, they decided to play charades. Renata and Jean formed a duo and seemed to be one and the same person. They were in perfect harmony, so much so that Charlotte and Homer eventually gave up. They didn't stand a chance against their opponents.

Just as the guests were leaving the house, Renata proposed staying with Jean to talk a little longer and reminisce about stories from their childhood. "Great!" Jean exclaimed, and Charlotte made no objection.

Jean no longer looked as sad as he had in the beginning. He and Renata sat next to each other, talking about the past. As they talked, they discovered that *Je t'aimais, je t'aime et je t'aimerai* by Francis Cabrel was their favorite song.

— Whenever I hear this song, I think of the letter you wrote me. This story was very funny — Jean said with a happy look on his face.

— It really was — Renata said, laughing heartily — Your parents were angry because they thought I was trying to interfere with your studies.

— That's right! They were trying to protect me.

— That's normal!

Since Renata knew what had happened to Jean's parents, she avoided talking much about them. So they talked about some other things all night, and out of the blue, they decided to go to Benin together with Charlotte and Homer.

At some point in the evening, Jean put their favorite song on replay. They both knew the lyrics by heart, and when it got to the chorus, they sang along, hugging each other:

Et quoique tu fasses
L'amour est partout où tu regardes
Dans les moindres recoins de l'espace
Dans le moindre rêve où tu t'attardes
L'amour comme s'il en pleuvait
Nu sur les galets

As Francis Cabrel says in this song, love is in every corner of space, everywhere you look, in the dreams you have, always falling like rain on the stones. And at that moment, a feeling of attraction developed between Renata and Jean. A few months after Renata returned to Rio, they started a long-distance relationship, and on vacations, they would meet somewhere in the world.

XXIX
Manifestation of a goal

In the 1980s, Karina decided to live with her boyfriend. At that time, it was frowned upon for a woman to live with her boyfriend without getting married first. Therefore, Clymène, Karina's mother, once told her, "My daughter, you are a pioneer. You were a flight attendant when women from families like ours didn't do that. Then you joined another religion, while everyone in our family remained Catholic. Now, you are living with your boyfriend. You really are a pioneer." Karina's mother was embarrassed to tell her friends and relatives that her daughter was living with her boyfriend. When they asked about Karina, she would answer, "Karina got married," and people, surprised, would say, "What do you mean? And we weren't invited?" Clymène would make up an excuse, saying, "It was a simple wedding!"

After living together for a few years, Karina broke up with her boyfriend. She was forty at the time and knew that women at that age in Rio were already considered old and would have difficulty in finding a serious partner. Single men over the age of forty usually wanted the company of much younger women.

Besides feeling unattractive, she also didn't feel fulfilled living there. In fact, she never managed to adapt to the Rio lifestyle. She always felt like a fish out of water, and she had known since her childhood that one day she would leave for another country. At the time, she did not know where to go and started to pay attention to her surroundings to see if there were any signs.

Formerly in Brazil, when one worked as a flight attendant or a teacher, it was possible to retire after twenty-five years of work.

Karina, then, started her retirement process at the age of forty-seven. This was a little difficult because of the country's bureaucracy.

Fortunately, her mother was there to help her. For several months, she would go to the National Institute for Social Security and say, "Good morning, I came here to see the progress of my daughter's retirement application. Here is the number." They would look it up and tell her, "This one is not finished yet, but we will take care of it soon." Some time later, she would return and insist, until one day she came to Karina and announced, "You got your pension!"

Karina saw her pension clearance as a sign that it was time to leave the country. The Inner Master told her, "You can leave now." She just had to decide where to go. One day, while walking in Copacabana, she noticed a young man with a T-shirt with the word "AUSTRALIA" written on it. This caught her attention and she thought, "Why not? Australia might be a good place to live."

Soon after that, she traveled to Australia. When she arrived in Sydney, she stayed in a Youth Hostel, a very simple and affordable place. She had a room to herself and was happy about this because privacy had always been a crucial thing in her life. In this hostel, she met several Koreans who wanted to learn English. They had great difficulty understanding the Australian accent and preferred to take classes with Karina, even though she was not a native English speaker. Since she also wanted to teach Portuguese, she put an ad in the newspaper. After a few days, some interested students showed up. These students told others about the classes and the group grew. In this way, Karina was able to earn a living through her classes while she was living in Australia.

The visa she had to enter Australia was valid for six months. Time passed rapidly, and soon she had to renew it. She had two options — renew the visa there or get a new visa in Brazil, taking the opportunity to be with her family. She went back to Brazil and, after getting her new visa, she decided to buy her ticket to Sydney. At that moment, something happened that changed the course of her life.

This event, besides being unexpected, was also spiritual. To better understand this, it is necessary to go back a little in time. As we know, a woman in her forties in Rio is usually considered too old to be attractive to men. Karina found herself in such a situation. She longed intensely to find the right person with whom she could share her life, and she knew that in Rio, this would be very difficult.

When she was living in Australia, she attended an event of Spiritual Freedom, where the speaker talked about the importance of setting goals in life. So, Karina started setting goals every day. One of her goals at that time was to meet the right partner with whom she could share the blessings of life. Every morning, she would write in a notebook, "I have a companion who helps me serve life." The interesting part about this statement is that even though she had no potential suitor, she set her goal with the verb in the present tense, as if it were already happening at that moment. By acting this way, Karina was creating molds that would be filled by a higher energy and manifested if she deserved it.

Her first partner, her boyfriend with whom she had lived in Rio, was a wonderful man, but eventually, they split up. Now, some years later, Karina had grown spiritually and wanted a different kind of partner — one who would help her to serve life.

When she got her Visa, the Inner Master suggested that she buy her return ticket for Australia at a particular travel agency. He told her, "Go to that agency and ask for the best Rio-Sydney ticket." In her mind, she answered the Master, "What do you mean? I already have a plan. The first time I went to Sydney, I went via the South Pole, and the ticket was the cheapest I could find. I think I'd better buy it with the same airline." The Master insisted, "Go to that particular agency."

The lady at the agency gave her several suggestions and then suddenly said, "We have a great promotion with Canadian Airlines."

Karina thought, "But it doesn't make sense for me to go from Rio to Sydney via Canada in the Northern Hemisphere."

The lady added, "It's an excellent promotion. Besides, you can spend a few days in Canada if you like. Have you ever been there?"

— No, I've never thought of going there.

— You could spend a few days there and then continue your trip to Sydney.

— I will think about it. I'll get back to you when I decide.

— OK. Great!

When Karina got home, she remembered that she had received an invitation from the Spiritual Freedom Path to a seminar in Montreal at the time she was planning to return to Sydney. She immediately thought, "That settles it, I'm going with Canadian Airlines. That way I can attend the seminar and then continue to Australia." During her stay in Canada, she met the man who was the manifestation of the goals she was setting. The Inner Master guided her to him.

XXX
The Inner Master

Karina, Vanessa, and Paulo were sitting at one of the patio tables in Café Sorriso. They were talking about various subjects. The sun was not so hot anymore, and from time to time, a soft breeze refreshed the air. At a certain moment, Vanessa asked Karina, "How long have you been married in Canada, madam?"

— Don't call me madam because it makes me feel old. It has been over twenty years.

— Sorry! I said "madam" out of respect — said Vanessa.

— Wow! Nowadays, staying married for more than twenty years is quite a feat — Paulo said, half to himself.

— Sometimes I ask myself about how we can tell if our partner is the right person. I wonder if there is a right person for each of us — Vanessa asked, looking at Paulo.

She and Paulo believed in the theory of Soul mates. That is why both were still fixated on the memories of their great loves that had not worked out. As a teenager, Vanessa had loved Thiago madly and since then had never fallen in love again. Paulo, on the other hand, no longer loved Renata, and yet he was still attached to the idea that his marriage to her could have worked out.

Karina replied, "I like to draw an analogy to my relationship with Erik, my husband, as if we were two full glasses. We add a full glass, which is me, to him, another full glass, and the result is two full glasses, existing independently of each other. Most couples we know are half-full glasses that need each other to reach a state of fullness. This codependency is not healthy at all."

— None of the couples I know are like you and Erik — Paulo said, thoughtfully.

— I think this is based on the false theory of Soul mates, where people believe they can only be fulfilled if they meet their better half.

Vanessa listened in silence. With a perplexed look on his face, Paulo remained silent. In their reflections, they were searching for a meaning to Karina's explanation. The latter realized that her interlocutors needed some time to understand what she had just said. She was quiet and just smiled. Finally, Vanessa broke the silence and said, "Thank you so much for sharing that! It makes a lot of sense. It feels good to know that we can be happy, not depending on anyone else."

— My pleasure! — Karina replied.

Vanessa continued, "Madam... Oh! Excuse me! Could you please tell us how you met Erik?"

— Certainly! I'd be happy to!

While listening to Karina, Vanessa discreetly, but noticeably, glanced at Paulo. This gesture told Paulo that he should turn the page with Renata, allowing the flower of love to grow again in his heart.

Karina began to speak.

— I met Erik when I went to a Spiritual Freedom seminar in Montreal, Canada. Since I was alone at that time and really wanted to find a partner, I set the following goal, "I have a partner who helps me serve life." During the seminar, the Inner Master said to me, "You have plans to stay here for a week, but one week is not enough." I immediately asked, "Why wouldn't one week be enough?" The Master replied that I would soon understand why. And I thought, "But I don't have enough money to stay here for a long time, just spending and not working." Finally, the Master said, "Find a way." I soon came up with an interesting idea. I wrote on a piece of paper that I would like to spend time with a French-speaking family to improve my French, and that I could exchange my stay for housework. Then I put the note on the bulletin board of the seminar. Half an hour later, there was already a name and a phone number on the piece of paper. I called the woman, whose name was Louise, and she immediately said that I could stay with her and her two teenage children as long as I wanted and that I wouldn't have to do any housework.

Karina paused for a while and continued — One day, she invited me to attend a meeting of our spiritual group. When we finished, I started talking to the people around me. At one point, I came up to Erik and said, "Hi, I'm from Brazil, and I'm spending a few days here." When we shook hands and I said, "Nice to meet you," I could read his mind, "What does this woman want from me?" There were many single women in that spiritual group, and Erik was one of the few men available. They would hit on him, and he would run away from them. When I introduced myself, he thought I was just another woman interested in him. The Inner Master immediately said, "That's enough! Now go talk to some other people."

Vanessa interrupted Karina, by asking, "Who is your Inner Master?"

— She has a strong connection with her inner world — Paulo answered in Karina's place.

— That's right, Paulo. This connection manifests itself as an inner voice that speaks to me, giving me guidance. Today I call it my Inner Master — Karina added.

Amazed, Vanessa exclaimed, "How interesting. I'd like to hear this inner voice."

— It's not a common thing — Paulo pointed out.

— It's not common, but it is possible — Karina said immediately.

They looked at each other quickly, and Karina continued telling her story.

— The following week, I went back to the same place for another activity. Since I had already understood that Erik didn't want to talk to me, I ignored him. Soon after, a lady named Yvette, who lived in the same building, came up to me and said, "Karina, I'd like to invite you over for tea, but don't tell anyone. I don't like to have too many people in my house. I only invited Erik because I like him very much." So, the three of us went to Yvette's for tea. While she was in the kitchen, I was chatting with Erik in the living room. I pretended to be indifferent so that he wouldn't feel uncomfortable. After tea, he took me to a subway station, and from there, I went to Louise's house. The next day, the Inner Master suggested I do something I don't usually do, "Call Erik." Louise, my hostess, had his phone number. Since he wasn't home, I left a message. He didn't call me back, but I saw him at the next spiritual meeting. At the end, he came over to me and said, "Sorry I didn't call you back. It was because I had a very busy day. But a group of friends and I are going out for a bite. Would you like to come along?" I readily accepted. After that day, the Inner Master told me that I should continue my trip to Sydney. I made the arrangements, and Louise decided to have a farewell dinner, inviting Erik. At this dinner, he asked me how I was going to get to the airport the next day. I had planned to take a taxi, but he offered to drive me before going to work. He drove me to the airport, and when we said goodbye, we exchanged our contact info, thinking that we would most likely never see each other again. Some time later, he started calling and faxing me. At that time, it was not very common for us to use the Internet. One day, he proposed over the phone. I was very surprised because I hardly knew him. But the

Inner Master gave me two signs. The first one was to show me that we had many things in common — we followed the same spiritual path, we weren't in a relationship, we were born in the same month, only six years apart. Then the Master added, "Why not say yes? If it doesn't work out, you can come back here or return to Brazil." The second favorable sign was a dream I had the following night. It was autumn in this dream, and I was in a place with colorful trees. In Sydney and Rio, the trees don't change color the same way. So, I thought, "This can only be in Canada." I decided to follow the Master's guidance and went to Canada, where we got married in the fall of that year."

Paulo listened quietly. Vanessa was the only one who asked questions. She had always been interested in adventures of travel and love. So she asked, "Was it that fast?"

— Yes, I met him in June. Then I went to Australia, and he proposed in July. I came back to live with him in Canada in August, and we decided to get married on October 22 at the temple of our spiritual path.

— How was the wedding ceremony? — Vanessa asked, curious.

— I didn't invite anyone, but many people attended. This was because a couple from Australia got married the day before, and their guests, who were also my friends, came to my wedding. And Ingrid, the woman who introduced me to the Spiritual Freedom, happened to be there in the temple too. She is a flautist and asked me, "Would you like me to play the flute at your wedding?" We loved the idea, and it was just wonderful.

— I can see that all of this happened because you listened to your Inner Master — Vanessa said, finding the story amazing.

— The Inner Master is a quiet voice that comes from the heart of each one of us. Sometimes it's a little difficult to perceive It, but when we open our hearts, It manifests Itself whenever we need It. The truth is that It is always with us. The question is, "Are we with It?"

Vanessa was amazed at the revelation of the inner voice. Paulo, who had been silent until then, finally said, "Could it be that the Inner Master is the best version of ourselves?"

— Absolutely! — agreed Karina.

It was about time for Café Sorriso to close. Vanessa's face expressed joy and gratitude at the same time. She thanked Karina for the story and asked permission to go and tidy up the place. A short time later, Paulo and Karina left Café Sorriso.

The next day, while Paulo was thinking about Karina's story, he remembered his son's invitation to attend one of his plays. He had received two tickets and thought, "Why not invite Vanessa?"

XXXI
A great African king

Homer went to Africa with Charlotte, Renata, and Jean. The plane landed in Cotonou, the financial capital of Benin. There they rented a car to go to Ouidah, a historical city, where they were going to stay at La Casa Del Papa Hotel.

On the way to the hotel, they stopped to walk around the *Temple of the Pythons* in Ouidah, where they took countless pictures. Renata really liked the icy sensation when she put the pythons around her neck. In Benin, culturally speaking, every foreigner is considered a king, so the Beninese treated Homer's friends like kings and queens. Renata and Charlotte were delighted to be there at that moment. At a certain distance from this voodoo shrine, they stopped again to look at another place. Together with a tour guide, they took the same route as the slaves did until they reached *The Door of No Return*. The slaves left for the Americas from this place, believing they would never come back.

The guide told them that most of the slaves deported to Brazil had left from Ouidah, and that many of them had returned as free men after the abolition of slavery. He said that in the city of Ouidah, there are many people with Brazilian names, descendants of the slaves who returned to Africa after a long time.

As they listened to stories about Ouidah, Renata, who knew very little about Benin until she met Homer, became emotional. Sitting on a rock beside *The Door of No Return*, she picked up a handful of sand, wondering if one of her ancestors had come from there. Like many Brazilians, she might have some African blood running through her veins. If this was true, she could consider herself part of that place, a beloved daughter of the city of Ouidah. In her short reverie, she realized that although the continents were separate, human beings were somehow all connected to each other. "The world is so small," she thought. Then she looked intensely at the sea, imagining the sadness it had experienced, seeing thousands of men and women being deprived of their freedom.

After showing them the monument, the guide ended by saying, "We are all one." Soon after, they made their way back to La Casa Del Papa Hotel, where they settled down in the utmost tranquility.

The hotel rooms were very cozy, despite being basic. From the windows, you could see the sea and the palm trees, whose leaves reminded one of freedom. Nothing could be more beautiful than that. From the balcony of her room, Renata looked at all this natural beauty. She felt at home because her proximity to the sea reminded her of the beauties of Brazil.

La Casa Del Papa was in a huge area, with a soccer field, basketball and tennis courts and mini-golf courses. There were also gardens, swimming pools and much more. To the right of where Renata was standing, the sea stretched endlessly. On the other side, a sizable lagoon could be seen resting with its still waters. In silence, Renata meditated on the incandescent green of that landscape, and in a strange way felt isolated from the world, as if she were on another planet, far from the noise and anxiety of the big cities she had already passed through.

While enjoying the refreshing air, she remembered that the hotel also offered a spa service. She invited Charlotte to go and relax. After a good massage session, they went for a walk with the boys. In the evening, they lit a bonfire near the hotel's lagoon. Other tourists joined them, and everyone was sharing stories until

Monsieur Mamandou arrived. He was the oldest Griot[2] in this historical town.

Monsieur Mamandou, who was of Senegalese origin, told them the legend of King Béhanzin, also known as *Kondo*[3]*, The Shark*. He was a great king who dedicated his entire reign to the fight against French imperialism. Finally, he surrendered to his enemies in order to avoid a war against his people.

Mamandou's singing and gesticulating brought the story of that king to life. It was so moving that some people cried. Renata saw, in the king's courage, the manifestation of unconditional love — a life dedicated entirely to the service of his people. She thought, "If today's rulers could love their people in this way, the world would surely be a better place."

Before that trip to Africa, Renata had never thought about social issues in such a profound way. Now she was about to rediscover another face of the world and perhaps a new version of herself.

---

[2] Griot: in parts of West Africa, someone who passes on their society's history, especially through stories, poems, and music, and who takes part in ceremonies such as weddings and funerals.
[3] Kondo, the shark is a Historical drama in 3 acts that describes the anti-colonial resistance of the Dahomean king Gbéhanzin. PLIYA, Jean, KONDO, LE REQUIN. Yaoundé: Ed.CLE, 2010.

XXXII
Beyond the horizon

Paulo was sitting in the middle of the audience, in a theater in Rio. He was looking enthusiastically at the stage. Next to him, was Vanessa. Ana Paula and her husband, as well as Renata and her boyfriend, who had come to spend a few days in Rio, were all in the theater. Bianca, Rafael's wife, was also there.

On the stage, you could see the set depicting the dawn of a new day and a tree as white as snow, symbolizing the purity of life. A woman came on stage holding a pitcher and sat under the tree. Reflective, she looked at the audience. Rafael, who played a soldier, entered the scene. When she saw him, the girl's heart leapt for joy, and she stood up to hug him.

Paulo took Vanessa's hand, and she did not withdraw it. Maybe it was because he was more than thrilled to see his son acting in his own play. With his hand clasping Vanessa's, he could not measure the joy in his heart.

In the play, the two characters were called Natalia and Glauber. Natalia was so beautiful that her presence intensified the stage lighting. Everyone could notice her splendor. Glauber remained still, holding a rose.

The play was about the mistaken belief that happiness is to be found outside oneself, beyond the horizon. Natalia tried to explain that we can find happiness in our hearts, but Glauber did not listen to her and left searching for that happiness somewhere else.

At the end of the play, Natalia received the news that Glauber had died in a tragic accident before reaching the destination of his dreams. She was sad, crying non-stop for days on end. Some time later, she found out that she was pregnant and that their love would survive in that child.

When the play ended, Paulo and Vanessa walked hand in hand. She did not hide her enthusiasm being in his company. He, for his part, felt a little uncomfortable, but said nothing about it. They waited for Rafael at the entrance to congratulate him. Vanessa wondered what the meeting with Paulo's family members would be like. Until then, she only knew them through what he had told her.

Ana Paula and her husband approached them, and Paulo introduced Vanessa. A short time later, Rafael appeared in the company of Bianca and Renata. When Paulo saw Renata, he discreetly let go of Vanessa's hand. Vanessa, smiling, said nothing, but was a little hurt. Renata noticed the stranger's presence and asked Paulo, "Aren't you going to introduce us to your friend?"

— Yes, of course! This is Vanessa, a colleague from my old job — Paulo said, trying not to pass on details of his friendship with Vanessa at Café Sorriso.

Renata was happy about her son's achievement, and with her face lit up, she smiled warmly at the stranger. Vanessa, although saddened by Paulo's behavior, did the same. Everyone congratulated Rafael for the beautiful play and his good performance. At some point, Vanessa's cell phone rang, and she asked permission to answer it. She left the theater and never came back. After a while, Renata said, "Paulo, don't you think you should go after Vanessa? It's been a few minutes since she left."

— You're right, I'll go look for her — Paulo said.

Vanessa had already left. Right after taking a taxi, her eyes were moist, and she shed a few tears. Life is like that — One day, dreams come true, the next, tears of disappointment are shed.

Vanessa and Paulo had been friends for eight years. The day they met, she felt something special for him. However, she was content with their friendship. Now, the fact that Paulo had taken her hand during Rafael's play changed everything.

Paulo called her that night, and they talked about what had happened. He said he didn't feel there was anything beyond friendship between the two of them. She replied that she had interpreted the situation in the wrong way and that she would rather distance herself from him.

XXXIII
A journey

One night, Paulo thought he would do something different before going to sleep. He sat down in a comfortable armchair and put his hands on his lap, as if he were about to receive God's blessings. He closed his eyes and put his attention on the third eye, a point between and slightly above the eyebrows. Then he did a Contemplation for the first time, totally engulfed in silence. This spiritual exercise made him so relaxed that he decided to do it every evening.

Karina had already said that Contemplation is a journey to our inner temple. She had also said that this kind of trip provides a very harmonious way to live. Now that Paulo had started contemplating, he noticed that his daily life became lighter and lighter. Moreover, he could tell when he got in touch with his inner world.

As time went by, he understood that he was no longer alone in the world, that something inside him was protecting him and guiding him to a higher purpose. It also didn't take long to realize that the more he practiced love in his actions toward others, the more his inner life grew stronger.

One day, when Paulo arrived home after talking to Karina, he didn't look for anything to eat. The conversation with her was enough to satiate his core and, consequently, his appetite for food. He then began to contemplate. At that moment, his thoughts became serene. They were limited to the present, completely free of the sorrows of the past and the aspirations for the future. Without realizing it, Paulo soon fell into a childlike sleep.

In the middle of the night, as his body lay unconscious in bed, his spirit began to wander in an unreal world. As Soul, Paulo found himself in a dream that seemed very real to him. He was walking through the streets of a city like Rio. With each step he took, he had the feeling he was in his own world, as if everything there was part of him, as if he was the creator of that dream. As he walked, he thought, "The buildings, the trees, the hills, everything here forms a unity with me."

Although he was in communion with everything, he still felt like a separate entity. He walked to the sand on the shore of a sleeping sea. It was dawn, and the wide sea covered the world, his world, the reality in his dream. At some point, his wandering eyes settled on the horizon and tried to find something different. However, there was nothing new there. In that place, there were only Paulo and the manifestation of his own world.

He sat down to contemplate the sunrise. The great bright star was moving smoothly over the horizon. From where Paulo stood, this giant star seemed to rise from the waters of the sea like a golden egg. The sea was no longer blue, for everything became luminous. Paulo's heart rejoiced, and momentarily, he heard a song coming from the ocean. While the gentle wind of that landscape sang the melody of love, the waves of the sea danced in total joy. Everything was perfect. Without any thoughts, Paulo understood his relationship with life and everything in it. He realized that the eyes of the heart see what is essential, which is only Love — that beautiful feeling equal to God, unchanging and always authentic, even when passing through several millennia and civilizations. Many have already been Its messengers, and others are yet to come. However, Love itself never changes, It always remains the same, in the present moment, capable of healing all afflictions and making existence a blessing.

Suddenly, a man in a maroon robe appeared at the edge of the sea. His luminous figure was interspersed with sunlight. He was dark-haired, with dark eyes and a refined goatee. The smile on his lips seemed never to have left his beautiful face. He was a majestic being, whose compassion moved the entire universe in this dream.

When they looked at each other, Paulo immediately felt a boundless joy conquering his heart, his inner world. He also had the feeling that the manifestation of that figure was the soft wind singing the melody of love in his ears. Paulo had heard about Spiritual Masters that appeared in people's dreams. He thought this bright being was one of them.

The stranger sat down next to Paulo and started the conversation as if they had been old friends.

— Long time no see, my friend. How are you?

— I'm fine, and you? — Paulo said in astonishment.

— I'm fine too. What have you been doing these past three years? — The man asked, smiling.

— A few months after my mother passed away, I was fired from my job. Since then, I haven't done anything.

— Have you forgiven yourself about your mother?

— I should have gone to visit her before she left. I can't forgive myself. It would be easier if I could go back in time — said Paulo, after thinking for a moment. — But what can I do about death? I already accepted that it is a necessary part of existence, and yet, it continues to be a mystery to me.

— My friend, I believe that death should not be much different from traveling from one place to another. Today you are here. If you travel tomorrow to another place, you will be absent from here. To die is also to be absent from earth, certainly going to a better place, suitable for the growth of each being.

— So death is a journey like any other? — Paulo asked, reflectively.

— If it isn't, we will know after we pass through it. In any case, there is no escape from it.

— It's true! — Paulo said with a more serene look.

— Make peace with yourself over your mother's death.

— I will.

— I must go now. And you must make your way back home.

Paulo, feeling that this being could answer all his questions, and not wanting to let him go, asked, "Who are we? Where do we come from? And where are we going to?"

The Master looked at him tenderly and said, "The less I ask, the more I hear the voice of silence — the song of the universe. The less I think, the more I contemplate the light of the universe — the word of the Great Soul."

Paulo listened, meditative. The mysterious man looked at him with love and continued, "Questions beget more questions, and consequently, no answer satisfies you." With his hand on his chest, he continued, "It's all in here, my friend", then said goodbye.

Soon after they embraced, the manifestation of the mysterious being disappeared into the soft dawn air. Instantly, the breeze that had played the melody of love in Paulo's ear blew again. After some time, he realized, in silence, that this melody was coming from within himself. Then he opened his eyes, finding himself back in his bed, back in real life.

He had just had a revelatory dream about one of the great mysteries of existence. He now knew that death was traveling from one place to another. Inside him, the fear of facing daily life vanished. He lay in bed at peace — a peace he had never felt before.

XXXIV
Return for a good action

When Karina got married in Canada, she did not want to depend financially on her husband. At that time, she earned a small pension from Brazil, which was not enough to survive in Canada. After reflecting a bit on her situation, she started to set a new goal for this stage of her life. Every day, she would write down her goal in the present tense as if her aspirations were already a reality. Soon afterwards, she got a job in a language school in Toronto. However, she didn't find this satisfactory because she was working a lot and earning very little. The interesting thing was that the school was constantly looking for teachers, not realizing that they dropped out because the pay was not good. The school paid Karina so little that one day her husband said, "You are spending more on transportation fares than they are paying you. I don't understand what you are doing there."

Whenever the Inner Master wanted to draw Karina's attention to some situation, the number 16 appeared. The day she finished the training course at this school, still in doubt about whether she should teach there or not, she saw the number 16 on the door of the cabinet where she would keep her material. Immediately, she realized that she had to go ahead with that job, even though it wasn't financially rewarding. Karina worked for this school for more than a year and had wonderful students. Unbeknownst to her, this job would help her résumé when she decided to apply for a job at the University of Toronto.

She kept writing down her goals in the present tense every morning, waiting for some other opportunities to arise. One day on the street, she saw an advertisement for a computer course that said, "Learn to make your own website." It was a course sponsored by the

Canadian government, and the enrollment cost was just twelve dollars.

After finishing this course, she created her own website on the Internet, posting personal and professional information. Having seen her website, a Brazilian man contacted her, asking for information about an English course at the University of Toronto. He had gotten the idea to ask her for help because, through the information on the website, he saw that she was an English teacher and lived in Toronto. He said in his message, "I loved your website, and I am planning to learn English in Toronto. Would you mind helping me get some information about the courses the U. of T. offers?" At first moment, Karina thought, "He could email the university himself, and they would reply for sure." As soon as she thought this, the Inner Master told her, "Help him!" She then answered his e-mail, "That's fine. I can look into it for you."

— Thank you!

— No problem!

On the same day, Karina called the U. of T. and left her request for information on a voice mailbox. She said she was Brazilian and needed details about the English courses for an acquaintance in Brazil. A few hours later, the general coordinator of the university's continuing education courses called her and provided the information she required. After this, she asked Karina if she knew anyone who taught Portuguese classes because the university needed to hire a Brazilian Portuguese instructor. Karina said that she worked as a professor in a language school and that she could help her. The coordinator then asked her to send her résumé with two letters of recommendation from good people.

In the first school where Karina worked, she taught one of the directors of a multinational company. He was learning Portuguese because he was going to be relocated to São Paulo. She remembered him and sent him a message, asking for a letter of recommendation. She got the second letter from the principal of the language school where she had worked. These two letters helped her to get the new job, which was a good thing in her career.

On the first day of class, Karina introduced herself as a Brazilian teacher. Most of the students were beginners, but there were some who were from Portuguese families and already had some knowledge. One of them said, "Miss, my mother is from the Azores. I want to learn European Portuguese."

— I'm sorry, I am Brazilian, and the university hired me to teach Brazilian Portuguese — Karina answered kindly.

At the time, the university did not inform people who enrolled in the course what type of Portuguese was taught. So, when Karina went home, she wondered how to solve this problem. The next day, she woke up thinking that it would be a good idea to strengthen her knowledge of European Portuguese. For many linguists, Brazilian Portuguese and European Portuguese are two different languages. They are both called Portuguese because Brazil was colonized by Portugal.

On the second day of class, Karina decided to meet the needs of all the students, and said, "Those who want to learn European Portuguese, please sit on the right side of the room. And if you prefer Brazilian Portuguese, please sit on the left side."

When Karina spoke European Portuguese, she tried to pronounce the words with the typical *"sh"* sounds. She explained the differences between the two languages, saying things like, "In Brazil we use *'você'* more often, and in Portugal, it's more common to use *'tu'*. And it went on like that for years.

To improve her European Portuguese, she watched the Portuguese news on TV. She would write down all the differences in vocabulary and pronunciation. She also decided to spend fifteen days in Portugal to perfect her skill in speaking European Portuguese.

Besides working for the university, she also had private students and could teach them in a more relaxed way. She could also meet the needs of each student according to the languages they already spoke. If the student only spoke English, she knew that the learning process would be slower. Those who already spoke a Romance language, such as Spanish or French, learned faster.

Karina paid a lot of attention to the students' difficulties and did her best to make them feel comfortable in class. Sometimes she taught grammar rules with playful activities, and the students liked her creativity very much.

Karina realized that living in service to life made her happy. In this way, she treated her students with respect and compassion, thus practicing the principles of the Spiritual Freedom in everyday life.

In fact, she was a person like any other, always looking for a way to earn her own bread. However, this external search did not hinder her process of self-knowledge. Ever since she was a child, she had heard the call of Soul, and never stopped searching until she found it in her own heart.

XXXV
The universe

A few kilometers from downtown Rio, on Ilha do Governador, Karina and Paulo were sitting on one of the benches at Tom Jobim International Airport. Karina was returning to Canada, and they were waiting for the departure time. Meanwhile, they took advantage of their last minutes together to say goodbye. From where they were standing, they could see people from all over the world, coming from one place and going to another.

Paulo said with a thoughtful look, "I have always been curious about you. I know that you travel a lot and have been to Europe several times, and I wanted to ask you how you get the money to go on these trips. I ask this because I know that you were an English teacher in Brazil, and everyone knows that teachers here don't make much money."

— Well, my retirement income was not enough when I moved to Canada, and I didn't want to depend on Erik financially. So I set myself the goal of earning a few extra bucks and surrendered it to the universe. I got some private students and a job at the University of Toronto. Furthermore, a few years later, I received a phone call from a Brazilian guy. He was one of my co-workers' husband. He asked me if I would like to co-produce an English teaching podcast. I told him that I preferred to create a podcast to teach Portuguese. At the time, he was a little skeptical about it because he thought we would not find anyone interested. So, I said, "We will never know if it is going to work if we don't try." He agreed, and soon we started producing some episodes. As this podcast was one of the first of its kind in the world, we enjoyed considerable success.

— That's great! And you became financially independent.

— Exactly! — Karina said, smiling. — Speaking of which, I remember that you had said in one of our conversations that you were unemployed and didn't know what to do. You could ask the universe for help, like I did. Who knows? Maybe it will show you a sign of what could be the next step in your professional life.

— Good idea! I could write down my goals in the present tense as if they were already accomplished. I remember this tip you gave me.

— This is a good way to manifest our dreams.

They agreed with a quiet laugh. Karina looked at her cell phone. She realized that there was not much time left before her flight boarded, and said, "Time to go!"

They got up, and Paulo said, "OK! Have a good trip!"

— Thank you very much!

— I will miss our conversations.

— Me too, but we can always talk by text or video.

— I'm glad we have this possibility nowadays.

Paulo gently took a rose with a note from his backpack and gave it to Karina. She was pleased and remembered that a few months before, while they were walking in Park Lage, she had bought him a rose with a note. Today, he was doing the same thing, consciously or unconsciously returning the love he had received months before. As they say about love — it is by giving that you receive.

Karina accepted the rose and, as she hugged Paulo, she whispered in his ear a sentence he had heard before, "Don't worry, everything will be fine." And they said goodbye. Paulo stood there, thoughtful about the future.

As Karina walked away, he felt butterflies in his stomach. This feeling of fear only lasted a few minutes, as he remembered Rafael saying that life is made of changes. Paulo then realized that every existing thing has a beginning and an end. At that moment, the uncertainty in his heart was gone, and in his inner world, a torrent of love and gratitude began to pour out for having met Karina.

He sat down, and quietly closed his eyes. Less than a minute passed before he opened them again. In a mysterious way, he found a world different from the one he had known until then. The airport itself appeared as the life, a two-way street, a road with no end and no beginning, a highway that crosses the world, passing through every corner of the Earth. Paulo also noticed the variety of passengers passing in front of him. They were of all types. Some smiled. Others did not. Some carried with them the passions of the mind, like anger and vanity. Others carried in their light hearts the virtues to cure these passions.

After this unusual and extraordinary experience, Paulo made his way back home. Somewhere along the way, he began to think about what Karina had whispered to him. He didn't know how to explain it, but he had the feeling that he had heard the same words before. He tried to remember when but could not.

High in the sky, Karina, sitting next to the airplane window, looked at the world below. Then she remembered Paulo's gift. She picked up the rose and read the note:

Before I met you,
I saw the colors of this world,
but I didn't know the light of my heart.
I listened to the sound of existence,
but ignored the music of my heart.
O friend of the world
I salute you with gratitude.

After reading this, she carefully put the rose and the note back in her bag. She began to gaze at the clouds and noticed that they were moving gently. Below the sky, the world seemed to have disappeared. At some point, she closed her eyes, focusing her attention on the third eye. She took a deep breath and felt an enormous joy welling up from within. Ecstasy became light in her vision, and she felt fulfilled for having helped a Soul remember Itself. By serving life, acting always with love, she had become a channel through which the universe operated. Although her encounter with Paulo seemed unusual, there was nothing coincidental about it. In fact, that episode was an important piece in Paulo's process of self-knowledge — an event that brought him the light and sound of Love in a critical moment of his life. Some time before, on one night when he was alone with his suffering, he looked into his bathroom mirror and wished that God would show him the way. And the Father of creation answered that call, using Karina's words to illuminate his son's steps.

Far away from the sky, in Rio, when it was time to go to sleep, right before he went to bed, Paulo did a Contemplation. While contemplating, he remembered the first time he had heard Karina's sentence, "Don't worry, everything will be fine." That had been a few months earlier, in a dream he had had when he was saddened by the events of life. When he remembered this, he saw his own existence as a work of God. He realized that the Absolute Soul was behind everything that happened in his life, always placing the right people, at the right time, on his path. He also understood that amid the difficulties of daily life, these people bring teachings necessary for everyone's evolution.

Somehow, Paulo concluded that Soul exists because God loves It, and that no being is apart from the Divine Plan. In this way, God is in everything that exists, and all things relate to one another.

In other words, the Absolute Father loves His children, and to consciously enjoy this unconditional love, we need eyes to behold His Light and ears to hear His Sound in the manifestation of the universe.

I sing because the moment exists, and my life is complete. I am not happy nor sad. I am a poet.
Cecília Meireles

XXXVI
Facing fear

After Karina's departure, loneliness became part of Paulo's everyday life again. However, he was no longer the same as before. Now he knew how to deal with this situation. He had learned that fullness was not to be found in relationships or in material things after the mysterious Master appeared in his dream. He remembered the words, "All that is needed is in the heart." In addition, he developed the habit of doing a contemplation every night.

He spent his days peacefully. He read a lot, and from time to time, went for walks on the beach. Now that his relationship with his family was in harmony, he called them frequently. He was in good terms with his father. Renata was happy with her boyfriend Jean, and Ana Paula continued not sharing her secret with anyone. Rafael won an international literary award with his book *The Poem of the Universe* and was now a well-known author. He and his little family were happy too.

However, there were two things that worried Paulo — what his next job would be and his estrangement from Vanessa. He was afraid to take risks, afraid to believe in new beginnings, afraid to love again, afraid to experience the delights of the present, not worrying about the hurts of the past.

One day, while walking on the beach, he remembered that Karina set goals for her life, and he got the idea to write to his Inner Master. When he got home, he wrote in a notebook, "Thanks to the Inner Master's guidance, I am doing something I love professionally, and I accept what is meant to be with Vanessa." He wrote these words every night. A few months passed, and one night he had a dream.

In the dream, he saw Karina. They were sitting on the same bench as always, in front of the sea. Karina said, "You could show your paintings in the Café Sorriso. It will make the atmosphere more romantic, and your poems will delight the customers." Paulo remained silent, not knowing what to say. Karina continued, "Who knows? Maybe you can become a great artist and earn some money with it."

— Can you imagine? Me, a great painter, and my son, a great writer and poet. People will think we are a family of dreamers — said Paulo, smiling.

— They say that life is generous with dreamers.

— Who knows? — Paulo murmured.

— It doesn't hurt to try — Karina said, satisfied, as she watched the infinite sea.

The first ray of sunlight came through the half-open window of his room. Paulo awoke at that moment and began to think. For all these years, he hadn't expressed what really made him happy — drawing and painting. He got out of bed and began to examine the painting at the entrance to the bathroom — *The Return*. He remained there, quiet, and meditative for a few minutes, but he still did not know what he had to do.

That morning, he began to tidy up his apartment as he thought about the answers to his two questions — he had to decide which direction to take in his professional life and whether he wanted to resume his relationship with Vanessa. Unexpectedly, his next-door neighbor put on a song called *Epitaph* by the Titãs. At the very beginning of the melody, the singer sang:

I should have loved more
Cried more, Seen the sun rise
I should have risked more
And even have made more mistakes
I should have done what I wanted to do

At that moment, Paulo was taken over by an unknown energy and then thought, "I should have painted the beauty of the world as I always wanted to." When he was a child, he liked to paint what the world offered to his innocent eyes. At that time, he didn't judge. He only depicted what the universe allowed him to see. He began to remember the good moments from his childhood, especially when he visited his grandparents on their farm. He remembered the feeling of watching the sunset; the river not far from the farm; the horse that soothed his sick grandmother; his first dog that loved him more than himself; the nights full of shining stars; the birds in the trees and in the sky; the crowing of the rooster that woke him up in the summer mornings; and the farm grass that was always green as a new beginning.

When the song ended, he thought, "Since the universe has always taken care of me, all I can do now is pay homage to it." Then he decided to go back to dreaming about life as he used to do when he was a child, back to being that boy who felt fulfilled when he contemplated the beauty of nature all around him and painted them. While trying to justify this decision to himself, he remembered his grandmother who once told him, "When you grow up, remember that God's flute plays in the hearts of children." Now, Paulo was an adult who was about to see the world with a child's heart.

That same day, after a thousand serene thoughts, he went to an art supply store and bought some canvases, acrylic, and oil paints. After returning home, he began to paint. From that day on, whenever he woke up in the morning, he painted what life inspired in him or what the dreams of the previous night had revealed to him. After a few days, there were already a dozen of beautiful paintings in his apartment. At the same time, he was painting, he was inspired to write some poems about love, justice, and beauty.

His most famous poem was:

O Soul that I am,
Truth that dwells in a temple.
Black or white wrapping,
Spirit that has no color.
Small or large body,
Conscience that has no size.
The atheist or believer,
Soul that is complete.
Beautiful or ugly face,
Passion that transcends perfection.
Bright or faded costume,
Soul whose heart is the sun.
O Great Soul,
Soul of all Souls,
You are everything, you are nothing.
Between the beginning and the end,
You are eternity.
Between lack and abundance,
You are contentment.
In euphoria and sadness,
You are serenity.
In the union of day and night,
You are the sunset and sunrise
— the Love that moves the temple.

After a while, he went to Cafe Sorriso to reconnect with Vanessa. They talked for a long time, and finally, he invited her to his home. There she saw the paintings and said very happily, "It would be wonderful to show these paintings at Café Sorriso. The space is large, and I believe they would add a new light to the atmosphere." They spent the whole night together and ended up making love.

A few years passed, and Paulo was now working as a painter and exhibiting his paintings at Park Lage and at Café Sorriso. At the end of each year, he and Vanessa would travel to different countries and enjoy more and more what the world had to offer. They went to places where Vanessa had already been, but the feeling for her was not the same, since now her chosen one was by her side. They eventually got married and invited Karina to the ceremony.

Over time, Paulo taught Vanessa how to do a Contemplation. She realized how delightful the journey to the inner temple is, which was enough for her to feel fulfilled. From then on, she no longer traveled to other places in the world to fill the void in her heart. She traveled only to discover the world, to see new things, to have fun and enjoy some adventures with her beloved.

Vanessa had now become a full glass of water next to Paulo, another full glass of water. The two loved each other but were not dependent upon each other for their happiness. They fully experienced the present moment, savoring the delights of each instant of their existence.

XXXVII
A blessing

A few years after getting married to Vanessa, Paulo woke up early in the morning in their new apartment in Copacabana. He got up and went to the window. Vanessa was still sleeping like an angel. Paulo looked at the street. The city was wakening up, with people gradually heading out to work.

He felt the touch of a breeze. It was the same gentle breeze that had made him go out years before, on the day he met Karina. He breathed in the fresh air of that spring morning and remembered his first conversation with his lovely friend. At that moment, he was overcome by a strange feeling, as if something inside was telling him to go to the beach. "It's probably a message from the Inner Master," he thought. Ever since he had begun to practice the exercises and principles of Spiritual Freedom, his connection with his inner world had become more and more intense.

He took his notebook and pen and went to the beach. As he walked, a stream of love came from within him like a divine waterfall. He noticed life flowing from his heart. He smiled and greeted the people who had gotten up early to go about their daily affairs. The city was slowly coming to life under a pale sun. Paulo thought of nothing else and walked in peace.

When he arrived at the beach, he saw a young woman sitting on a bench. He didn't know why, but something led him to her. He sensed that he had to talk to that woman, but hesitated a bit. In big cities, people are usually suspicious and do not open to strangers.

However, the Inner Master silenced the doubts in his mind, telling him, "Go and talk to her." Paulo approached her and said, "I have walked a lot today. May I sit here and rest for a while?" She nodded in agreement. He sat down, took his notebook and pen from his backpack, and began to draw the beautiful landscape before them.

Paulo and the stranger were there, sitting on a bench in front of the infinite sea. She was deep in thought, and he was sketching in his notebook. A few minutes passed, and a couple, walking hand in hand, passed in front of them. Upon seeing the couple, the woman began to cry. Noticing this, Paulo said in a soft voice, "There is no more magical spectacle than the sunrise and sunset. Did you see the sunrise?"

Quietly, the girl glanced at him and began to look at the surrounding landscape. The bright sun was filling the horizon, turning the surface of the sea golden and blue at the same time. A light breeze came up, causing the palm trees to sway. Life was manifesting itself in nature, and anyone there could see this.

After a while, looking at the surrounding landscape, the woman stopped crying. She took a deep breath and asked Paulo, "Why do you think the sunrise and the sunset are magical moments?"

— Because the night and the day become one, and I feel the presence of God — answered Paulo.

The girl smiled in agreement, saying, "I have never realized that before. Thank you for reminding me that we can still find God in the manifestation of nature."

— My pleasure! It also took me many years to finally realize that there are divine things happening around us all the time.

— True! — said the woman, wiping the tears from her face.

At that moment, the Inner Master said to Paulo, "Now you can go home."

Paulo said goodbye and left. Deep inside, he was happy that he had managed to raise a smile in someone. That smile could make the woman's heart lighter. The truth is that he only wanted to help, and in doing so, he did the same as Karina, who always made herself available to listen to him when he needed most to talk. Now he was doing the same with other people, not getting attached to the results of his action.

As he walked home, he was sure that everything in the universe was connected. Somehow, he felt linked to that woman as well as to Karina. He knew he was not wrong, for if all existence came from one thing, the essence of creation must be found in everything. With this realization, Paulo concluded that it was no accident that he had gone to the beach so early in the morning for no apparent reason. He had to be there because that woman needed to be reminded that God exists and is always by our side in good and bad moments.

As Paulo thought more about what had happened, he noticed the generosity of life. In the blink of an eye, existence seemed to him like a vast school with millions of classrooms. Their corridors were many roads that spanned the face of the earth. Their lessons and tests were infinite, and in each classroom, were masters and disciples to teach and learn. When one lived, one had to be in tune with oneself to realize when to learn or teach, and when to speak or listen. Soon after realizing all this, Paulo found himself in front of his building. He went up to his apartment and lay down. Vanessa was no longer there. She had already left for Café Sorriso.

The woman was still sitting on the bench near the beach. After a while, she went to the sea and got her feet wet. She looked at the ocean without thinking, noticing the sound of the wind. She became one with everything there. The sea and the wind were now a part of her. After a moment, she felt again like a separate entity. The vast sea seemed to reach beyond infinity, and the wind seemed to come from far away.

The waters came and went, wetting her feet. She raised her eyes and noticed that the sea now resembled life. Its waves could rise in fury or subside in tenderness, the sea always remained the same, unchanged, and infinite. "I am the ocean, I am everything," she thought, and soon realized that neither joy nor sorrow could prevent her fulfillment. If the sea does not surrender to either calm or angry waves, why would she surrender to the circumstances of life? After meeting Paulo that day, she discovered a new way of living.

After her reverie, she bent down and picked up a handful of sand. She started to walk along the water's edge, looking at everything around her, until her gaze landed on the Sugar Loaf Mountain, which seemed to touch the bright sky. She then realized that God's glory is not so far away from earth. At that moment, she experienced a joy she had never felt before. She was fulfilled and happy, knowing that life is a blessing.

THE END

Author's Instagram: @herlicpoemas

CPSIA information can be obtained
at www.ICGtesting.com
Printed in the USA
BVHW082204130922
646893BV00010B/702